CROSS CURRENTS

Janet age 14.

CROSS CURRENTS

A CHILDHOOD IN SCOTLAND

Janet Teissier du Cros

TUCKWELL PRESS

François Teissier du Cros and Janet's children wish to express their
deep gratitude to all their cousins and friends who gave their invaluable
help in preparing *Cross Currents* for publication

First published in 1997 by
Tuckwell Press Ltd
The Mill House
Phantassie
East Linton
East Lothian, Scotland

The publisher acknowledges subsidy from the
Scottish Arts Council towards the publication of this volume

ISBN 1 86232 069 1

A catalogue record for this book is available upon request from the
British Library

Typeset by Carnegie Publishing Ltd, Preston, Lancs
Printed and bound by Cromwell Press, Broughton Gifford, Wiltshire

C O N T E N T S

ILLUSTRATIONS

F O R E W O R D

Janet Teissier du Cros (1905–1990) was the fifth daughter of Sir Herbert Grierson, the first holder of the Regius Chalmers Chair of English which I occupy and one of the founding fathers of the modern subject we call English studies.

She may have been the most remarkable of the five sisters in her varied accomplishments, and was certainly a dutiful daugher, wife, mother and author. Her first book, *Divided Loyalties* (1962), embraced these roles and demonstrated her mettle as a writer faithfully chronicling her wartime activities in occupied France. *Cross Currents*, now posthumously published for the first time, follows its predecessor's lucid presentation of a society steeped in the contradictions of hierarchy and freedom, tradition and innovation.

The Griersons were a precocious Scottish family by any measure, consisting of father who was a trailblazing scholar steeped in his books and lectures, mother dedicated to her five girls and the running of her very sociable professor's household into which she injected an air of competitiveness and the sense that despite such parents the daughters would have to scale their own heights. All this among the cobblestones of Old Aberdeen – the ancient ecclesiastical village surrounding St Machar's Cathedral and King's College – and, later on, in King's Gate on the western edge of 'new Aberdeen'.

Janet's first ten years (1905–15) in Aberdeen are portrayed in a velvet-cushioned world of Edwardian teas and social visits. Still she sees darkly into its obliquities and dissects its complexities with the precision of a hawk's eye. Not even in quaint Aberdeen before the Great War was everything so sedate and cosy as seemed on the surface.

The Griersons moved to Edinburgh in 1915, after the start of war when Sir Herbert took up the Chair of English there after George Saintsbury's departure. Suddenly the ten-year-old Janet's world was turned upside down. The transition to Edinburgh proved one of the most memorable, if jolting, events of her life. The move, the two cities, their differences, form the pillars of this extraordinary memoir: Aberdeen and Edinburgh seen through the eyes of a gifted Edwardian adolescent.

The contrasts of the two cities are stunningly portrayed – they still resonate a century later. Aberdeen the more aristocratic of the two: proud, discreet, isolated, hierarchical, steeped in a timeless setting almost untouched by the outside world. Bustling and exotic Edinburgh the national capital: diverse categories of people everywhere, nationalities other than Scottish, almost another country from the spited Aberdeen Janet had vacated.

In Edinburgh the teenage Janet blossomed and developed her considerable talents in music. Here she circulated among such notable personalities as André Raffalovich, the eccentric Russian Jewish émigré who had been a friend of Oscar Wilde in Paris, and John Gray, the Anglo-Irish cleric and real-life 'Dorian Gray'. Janet excelled all the girls at school, cultivated the friendship of adults, especially W.B. Yeats, who admired her, and – somewhat *through* adults – formed her character for the future. Her father paved the way for her to take piano lessons with Donald Tovey, the Professor of Music at the University of Edinburgh, soon to become one of Europe's foremost musicologists. In this visionary company of older, and often distinguished, men the precocious Janet established her own identity and polished her individual talent.

Foreword

This is a period piece, sculpted along the lines of rooms with gilded views and the remains of innocence. Throughout, the narrating voice combines candour with restraint, and captures a world that must be of great interest to readers who inhabit these cities and ponder their social pasts. This memoir will go a long way, I predict, towards kindling a sense of wonderment about Aberdeen and Edinburgh as places with distinct cultural identities before and during the Great War.

The author has brilliantly remembered her girlhood impressions and woven them into memories accumulated over a lifetime in several countries and encompassing two world wars. The result is an almost Jamesian amalgam of youth and maturity, timeless in its vignettes, bearing not the slightest trace of nostalgia or sentimentality. Few memoirists have presented the social pulse of the era so elegantly – in the unassuming first-person voice of a teenage girl – yet with such microscopic insight and scrupulosity of detail.

George Sebastian Rousseau,
Regius Professor of English,
King's College Aberdeen
Spring 1997

To begin with, I have no exaggerated idea of the interest my memoirs can have for anyone except my descendants, but I do believe there may be some point in capturing and pinning down my version of the tail-end, which was all I knew, of a period during which a small part of the world lived in comparative security, at least on the level of private life. Today the dikes are down and the sea is pouring in and already even to my generation the magical oasis that was once so familiar looks dim and unreal. Yet my backward looking is not nostalgic because I believe that, at the moment of writing this introduction (1990), we are being given the dream of a far better world than we have ever known. Perhaps my attitude is nearer to that of the collector.

I believe that no one who was born even ten years later than I can have any notion of what in our time, country and class, security meant. I remember how shocked I was as a child to discover that though of the "top nation", not being aristocratic we were not of the top social level. The knowledge made a first fissure in my feeling of security; but it soon healed in the atmosphere of inviolability that surrounded us. Before even I heard the word "security" I knew that in the daylight at least we were safe; safe from hunger, from contempt, from snakes of the deadlier kind, from carnivorous beasts, and even from wars since wars were fought overseas. Not even motor accidents threatened us; motor cars were few and we had none. The remaining panoply of weapons known as "Acts of

God" was a restricted one at that time, on our proud chill island in the North Sea.

To this day, after what could be called a lifetime of living in France as a French citizen, I am still occasionally possessed of a devil. I think of her as British Subject. Her seed was sown in me, not in our home atmosphere, but in the wartime ambience of those early years, in the air we breathed at school, the history we were taught, the patriotic doggerel we were made to recite. I say nothing of the intimate bonds that bound us to Scotland, whose essence for me is the smell of bog-myrtle and of pine-needles. These bonds have nothing to do with nationalism, nor even patriotism.

However that may be, British Subject grew to full stature when in 1923 I first went abroad and discovered on the one hand what was even then the extent of British prestige, and on the other the extraordinary protection extended to all British subjects living abroad. I was in Vienna once during a Putsch. It was in 1929. Or was it 1928? There had been anti-semitic riots in the University, though it was before Hitler's day, and an attempt had been made to set the Rathaus on fire. Not knowing there was trouble in the city, I went out as usual to lunch in a restaurant and got caught in a hysterical running mob in front of the Opera House. I made my way home with some difficulty, greatly alarmed at having heard a shot or two, and had scarcely recovered my breath when the door-bell rang. I went to answer it and found a politely enquiring attaché from the British Embassy on my doorstep, come to ascertain that I was keeping my head.

There was to come a time when if anything occurred to rouse my moral indignation when abroad, then British Subject would fly to my rescue. She would speak through my lips with the voice of Empire and she would leave me feeling good. She never comes now. On the last occasion when she came, before she had finished talking, I knew myself for a fool.

I mention British Subject because she was the crystallisation of the sense of security and superiority I mentioned earlier. Today when I look back it seems incredible that I should have lived happily in mid-ocean on an ark past whose windows so many drowning bodies floated. The truth is that I never looked out. Surrounded as I was by kindly people, I believed that as a nation we could do no harm. It was not, for example, till I was in my thirties and read *The Great Hunger* that I learned the truth about Ireland. I was to have other shocks, or at least surprises, when it came to hearing my children recite their History lessons from a French manual; but all through my childhood and beyond I never questioned the Holy Plan that had set us as a family on the safe hard pinnacle of rock (to change my metaphor) round which the sands shifted. I took for granted that everything was ordered to some inevitable pattern.

This sense of security had its shadow side. By uttering magical formulae: "there are no wolves in Britain", "there have been no invasions since 1066", our mother banished behind iron bars our more rational fears; but when night came, loosing more occult foes, we were left helpless in a world where anything could happen. The latest murder story would rise from the kitchen and reach us through whispered conversations between nurse and housemaid. There was a brief period when I slept with the bedclothes pulled smotheringly about my face and throat and again and again I would run my hand down my neck to make certain no murderer had surreptitiously slipped a noose round it to be drawn tight the moment I fell asleep. When I came to have a room of my own I never got into bed without searching for a hidden enemy. In the end it was a purely mechanical gesture. I expected nothing. But there came a night when I was seventeen and came home late from a dance feeling so light-hearted and happy; from mere habit I cheerfully began my automatic ritual by casually opening the wardrobe door as a likely cache for a thief. Out leapt the large black family cat and if it had dug its claws into my heart the shock could scarcely have been greater. As it was, it cured me once and for all of the habit.

In Scotland there were also ghosts to contend with. Our connection through our father with the Shetland Isles gave us access to a rich store of uncanny tales which were enjoyable enough by firelight while chestnuts roasted between the glowing bars of the grate and exploded aptly at flesh-creeping moments. But once in bed the pleasure was gone. At the creaking of a floor-board or the rustle of a curtain my heart would pound and my scalp tighten till at last the very violence of my fear gave me the nerve to brave it. Out of bed I would leap and fly downstairs to my mother's room for succour. Patiently my father would leave the warm bed to end the night in his dressing-room, while I crept into his place beside my mother. The feeling of security that had ebbed with the daylight would then return. Warm as a feather-bed, wrapping me around and bearing me up, a buoyant yet solid feeling of safety which like a flying carpet carried me at last out of the fearful world of night and spilled me over into deepest sleep, to wake at last into the familiar world, secure.

PART ONE

Gaslight

THESE MAY NOT BE THE FACTS.
IT IS WHAT I REMEMBER.

CHAPTER ONE

Christmas Day

"Noël est un massacre!" The words spoke themselves in my head with sudden violence as I stood in the butcher's shop, rue Vaneau, one Christmas Eve many, many years ago. All around me were corpses – great hampers of geese and turkeys, dead and ready for trussing; long parallel spits turning and turning before a red glow of gas, each with its sizzling row of chickens, ducks and guinea-fowl, in preparation for the festivities that follow upon Midnight Mass; banal everyday corpses too, beef, mutton and veal, hanging from their cruel hooks. Peace on earth, goodwill towards men, but in the farmyard: death.

Not so was Christmas long ago when I was a child. Not in Aberdeen where I was born. Christmas then was life's focus and it penetrated my consciousness by a series of magical shocks too early for the earliest to subsist, so that in retrospect I see my childhood as suspended on a tense and glowing thread of expectation of Christmas Day.

The long period of waiting began the moment we reached home after the summer holidays. Lingering for a moment in the little front-garden where a candid line of asters had been drawn in place of the clumps of sweet-smelling wallflower, perhaps it would be the transient whiff of damp leaf-mould that suddenly made me skip. Not that I knew then that Autumn is the town-dweller's season of renewal. I had no notion what ferment was at work. I knew the world of the mind chiefly as "school"; and it was not the prospect of school that caused these inner spurts of joy. But at the breath of Autumn came the thought that though summer was over we could now start counting the days till Christmas.

The days passed slowly, but they passed. Soon the great wych-elms stood stripped of leaves under our night-nursery windows and in the back-garden only the michaelmas daisies lingered on. Long periods of wind and rain broke against occasional fine days when we could swish delightfully ankle-deep in drifts of damp autumn leaves. Excitement began to flag; we were back at school and it had lost the brief charm of novelty. Then, just as our world seemed to be holding its breath in an interminable hush of monotony, prosaic signs began to appear to remind us that a magnet was drawing all things to it. They appeared in the shop-windows and on the theatre hoardings and soon we could touch with our finger the first of the constant elements that keep chaos at bay and on which children build their sense of security; for the D'Oyly Carte Gilbert and Sullivan Opera Company was announced as being about to open its season in our city.

It is true that Gilbert and Sullivan have nothing to do with Christmas on the logical level, but the yearly timing of their visit made of them a sign. It meant to us that the solstitial orchestra was tuning up. We were always taken to one performance and for days beforehand we thought and talked of little else. We were as yet untouched by the intellectual snobbery which was later to ruin our enjoyment of Sullivan's tuneful nonsense, and it is a pity that any such confusing of levels as the judging of *Patience* or *The Yeomen of the Guard* by the standards of *Don Giovanni* or the *Meistersinger* should be allowed to trouble the minds of the young. Left to themselves they will learn to distinguish soon enough. The Gilbert and

Sullivan operas, for so long as we were allowed to enjoy them with a quiet mind, were fraught with magic. There were the actors with all of whom we were prepared to fall in love. There was the delightful familiarity with the music which we soon acquired, and above all there was the association with the Christmas season. It was as though from one Opera season to another, from one Christmas to the next, none of our enjoyment was ever lost but sank down through the layers of our consciousness to join an accumulated store of happiness which would well up on each new occasion and flood our hearts with delight.

And so through the shortening days the tension rose till at last the cycle was complete and it was once more Christmas Eve. Memory carries me back to an occasion when I must have been about eight years old. After a bad start I was just beginning to have glimpses of what a real relationship with my sisters could be, and on that evening the harmony was total between the three youngest of us who set out before tea to hunt for holly to bedeck the house. King's Gate where we lived, if in those days you followed it far enough, gradually dropped its town trappings and subsided into a country road between dark naked fields with an occasional farmhouse beyond. There was no snow that Christmas. As I remember things there was seldom snow; but a white hoar frost glistened on every blade of grass and petrified the landscape to silence. Ahead of us the sky had turned azalea-red and the hard frosty road seemed to be leading us straight into the setting sun. We followed it, tingling with cold and excitement and carrying between us, turn and turn about, an optimistic two-handled clothes-basket which we dreamed of bringing home laden with red-berried holly branches. Happiness is an immeasurable thing, but I do know that evening was one of the occasions when its tide ran highest.

At last we were brought up short by the sight of some holly-bushes by the wayside, or what we took for holly, and we turned aside to fill our basket. I remember my disappointment at there being no red berries. For the first time the thought took conscious form that nothing was ever quite right in Scotland: summers were never hot, no snow lay on the ground at Christmas, and now it seemed that there were no red berries on the holly. The burning beauty of the wintry sky I took for granted. I thought the sun set in the same glory the whole world over and counted it no whit to Scotland's credit.

And so at last the great day dawned, not necessarily the Christmas Day that followed on that Christmas Eve but any Christmas. Memories come crowding in. There was the very early Christmas when rich cousins had sent us a musical-box and we trooped into the drawing-room to its unreal tinkling version of "Hark the Herald Angels Sing".

Many many years later when I was a young married woman living in Marseilles, and the mother of two small boys, I went one Christmas Eve to call on an aunt by marriage who lived in Endoume, a Marseilles suburb. As I passed down the street that led to her house I caught through a window the sound of children's voices singing that very carol and I stopped to listen, pressing my ear as close as I dared to the curtained window. I was in a happy mood. At home my Christmas tree was waiting to be decorated and the toys were all ready for the children's stockings. It was from no feeling of nostalgia but rather to give an edge to my sense of enjoyment that I paused to listen to the familiar tune. Then suddenly my happy mood crashed and was shattered. I had caught the actual words and they were English words, and these were English children that plucked so mercilessly at the earliest emotional fibres of my being. All, all I had so cheerfully renounced when I first turned my back on Scotland and my face to France, nor ever once regretted, all now pulled at my heart-strings, waked by the melody that flowed – not very melodiously – from these children's throats: my family, my country, my friends and last but not least (it now seemed to me) the right to be myself and not forever an unwilling representative of the British people. I found myself in tears.

But on that earlier Christmas afternoon "Hark the Herald Angels Sing", as tinkled out by the new musical-box, was innocent of undertones. Its only perfume was the incense that rises from candle-wax, tangerines and resinous fir-needles. At the foot of the tree sat three baby dolls fully clad in flannel "barrycoat" long muslin gown and white woollen cape and bonnet. I guessed one of them must be for me, as was soon confirmed, and I ran to thank my mother. She said I must thank our Swiss governess too, who had made all the clothes by hand. "By hand" meant nothing to me, but I soon discovered it meant that the clothes all buttoned and unbuttoned instead of being sewn on, and so respect for craftsmanship was born in me before even I could manipulate buttons for myself.

Then there was the Christmas morning when, hanging round the drawing-room door behind which the last touches were being given to the Christmas-tree, we caught a glimpse of our father wearing his red-lined dressing-gown inside out so that if we glimpsed him we might take him for Father Christmas. We made no such mistake but we kept silent, amused at his not knowing that Father Christmas had nothing to do with the Christmas-tree. It was reserved for the presents given us by our parents and relatives. Father Christmas's job was to come down the chimney and fill our stockings.

I think that as the youngest of the family I learned fairly early that there was no such person, but I cannot remember feeling anything more than a passing regret. It had not the effect of shaking my faith in anything at all. Out of an odd loyalty to our mother we never spoke our disbelief but went on writing every year our letters to Father Christmas and putting them at the foot of the chimney last thing on Christmas Eve. The only result of my initiation – I refuse to call it a disillusionment – was that though we stretched our requests to the utmost bounds of possibility we avoided asking for the impossible.

Actually the presents we found in our stockings had value especially as focal points for our imagination, pegs on which to hang our dreams. It was the long rising crescendo when it burst into a tutti on Christmas morning that shed glory on all it reached.

Our mother had instinctive poetic knowledge of the importance of ritual or ceremony to life: the story always told in the same words, the red-letter day whose ordering of events is preordained, the Christmas stocking whose contents are linked by such constant elements as I referred to earlier. It was a long black woollen stocking that each hung on her bedrail on Christmas Eve and found the next morning long before sunrise comes to the north of Scotland in December, distorted and extended into something "rich and strange". Light-headed from lack of sleep, we drew its treasure out to be examined and exclaimed over, impatient to see whether our requests had been granted; but with, too, the safe under-lying expectation of these constant elements, the chocolate Father Christmas, the tangerine, and in the toe of the stocking the bright new penny.

The whole of the day was ordered to a ritual. Although as a rule we children grumbled at having to go to Church, on that day we were willing enough. After breakfast and a margin of time in which to arrange our presents, each on a tray or small table, we followed our mother along the frosty pavement to the tramcar stop in the delightful twilight of a northern winter morning. Inside my woollen glove I grasped the new penny and a half-crown postal-order sent me by my godfather, confident that more would be added in the course of the day by our grandfather and perhaps by one of our uncles. To us money too was material for dreams. Perhaps that is what it is tó misers. Apart from our weekly penny not much of it came our way and the possession of even a small sum opened up a fabulous world of possibility. It seemed to me that for so long as the money remained in my keeping it would buy all of the objects for one of which it would have been sufficient. For that reason, when I found myself inside the shop where I intended to spend it I could never make up my mind. I hesitated and hesitated, to the distress and shame of whoever accompanied me; for then I knew that I must choose, and it was as though by choosing I lost far more than I acquired.

One Christmas brought me when all was told the to me tremendous sum of four shillings and sixpence. This would allow me to buy a thing I longed for, a new set of furniture for the dolls' house which was one of the chief joys of my childhood. My mother took me to spend it in Union Street, the main shopping-centre of Aberdeen. She found herself once more faced with my difficulty of decision but she was unaware of its present cause. I had no doubt at all this time which of the sets of furniture I wanted, and its price would leave me with a shilling for other things. Unfortunately it happened to be a more complete version of some furniture Alice and Letty had recently clubbed together to buy for the dolls' house they shared. I must explain that there was a complex code of honour in vigour on our nursery floor. It was forged in tears and anguish but it gained strength as we grew older and saved us from much bitterness as we grew up. Its unconscious purpose was to avoid rivalry. By its law copying and trespassing on each other's preserves were prohibited. I therefore knew I had no right to buy that furniture, but I so longed for it that I would scarcely look at the other sets I was shown; yet neither could I bring myself to say that I would buy it.

I did at last unfold my problem to my mother, but the rules invented by children are things whose importance no grown-up can grasp. She said it was all nonsense and that Alice and Letty had no right to object to what I bought with my own money. I knew they had every right, but I knew too that my mother's patience was fast ebbing and so I bought the furniture. I bought it and I set out for home with no joy in my heart at all. And when we reached home things turned out exactly as I had known they would. I tried to smuggle the furniture into my dolls' house without my sisters discovering what I had brought home, but they very naturally crowded round, curious to see what I had got. And then there arose the hideous dreaded cry: "Copy-cat! Copy-cat!" they shouted in their fury. I could as little forgive myself as they could, though I tended to unload responsibility by inwardly blaming my mother for not having understood my predicament. Even my sister Flora, the second of the family, who often rose in my defence and who in theory shared the dolls' house with me though in practice she had lost all interest in childish games, even she felt that on this occasion I had done the wrong thing. A black mist closed in on me, as so often it did in those early years.

But I have left us all in the tramcar, jolting and swaying on our way to church. We had a long way to go. St. Margaret's episcopal church, which we attended, stood in the slum quarter of Aberdeen, as to their credit the episcopal churches of Scotland so often do. It was to me alarming territory, not only because of the occasional huge rat, scuttling to shelter in some dark nook, with a world of terror on its back. Even more it was the children that frightened me. Sometimes barefoot, often red-headed, their bold eyes and rough speech proclaimed in uncouth, incomprehensible terms that here they stood on their own ground.

And so home at last, after a triumphant "O Come All Ye Faithful", sung in Latin by Molly and Flora, our prodigious elder sisters; home for the great event of the day, the turkey (innocent in our minds of any connection with a butcher's shop), the plum-pudding and the Christmas-tree, all of which were shared by Auntie, Uncle Henry, Cousin Nel and Cousin Harry, our mother's aunt, uncle and cousins. Molly and Flora would have more to tell about Auntie than I, for they saw much more of her and at a more lucid age. Molly was her favourite, as Flora was Cousin Nel's, and both of them often stayed in the big granite house in Old Aberdeen over which she ruled. It stood in a large garden and is connected in my mind with sweet-peas and pansies and with helping Cousin Nel to saw wood for the summer fires and gather eggs in the wired-in hen-run.

I remember Auntie as a lively old lady wearing one of those black bonnets old ladies wore in those days, and who inspired me with awe because of her caustic tongue. Much later I was told she had played an essential part in my parents' meeting and marrying. From the age of five, when her real mother died, my mother was ruled, not without protest, by a stepmother who resented her beauty and kept her in the nursery with the younger children till she was twenty-seven, at which point, my father having been appointed to the first chair of Rhetoric and English Literature at King's College, Auntie sensed a match to be made and invited her favourite niece and the new professor to dinner. She even, when the time was ripe, manoeuvred an opportunity for my father to propose, to my mother's great distress, whose acute sense of modesty made her feel that her aunt was exposing her cruelly. My father reassured her when she attempted to escape from the room, explaining that he had asked her to procure him just such an opportunity.

When I was a child I took people at the valuation offered and considered those my parents loved as an extension of themselves. I therefore loved Auntie; but I was never really at ease with her. No one that lacked a sense of humour could be at ease with Auntie and my own only began to develop at the age of nine. I remember her once bringing me for my birthday a tin of chocolate-coated "puff cracknels". I never cared for puff cracknels, chocolate-coated or otherwise, my tastes were more voluptuous; but when Auntie handed me her present (I can still see her seated on one side of the nursery fire and old Nanny on the other) and said: "I have brought you biscuits because you and I disapprove of sweets!" what could I do but seem to acquiesce?

It was some years before I came to realize that Auntie had trials to bear of a nature to turn a lively wit caustic. Not the least of them must have been her husband, our Uncle Henry, a bumbling old professor of Theology who remains inseparable in my mind from black snow-boots and a white woollen muffler. He retained throughout his life a childlike innocence which must have been a sore source of irritation to Auntie's practical mind, but which had its charm. My father often told me how Uncle Henry and Auntie used to give each year a dinner-party for the latest batch of theological graduates with a view to preparing them, for they came as a rule of simple backgrounds, for the social side of the life that was opening before them. No detail was neglected, but as Auntie and her husband were both confirmed teetotallers it was not wine but ginger-beer that the maid poured into the crystal champagne glasses. Uncle Henry's students were in some ways as innocent as himself, and one of them once remarked to my father as they left the house: "Excellent champagne the Professor serves!"

Uncle Henry was moreover an exceptionally clumsy man who tended to upset whatever came within his reach. This clumsiness was aggravated by his having at some time lost the middle finger of his right hand. Auntie, who was a rare house-keeper and delighted in a certain sober domestic elegance, must often have suffered. I have seen him knock his newly boiled egg from its cup by some clumsy movement, and then, in his desperate efforts to retrieve it and avoid an acid repri-mand, bat it twice up into the air and twice catch it before finally it came crashing down on the clean table-cloth.

He had a strange yearning after every bottle of medicine that caught his eye; for though as far as I know he enjoyed excellent health he had a notion it would be better still if only he could drink their contents. "Don't you think a little of that would do me good, my dear?" he would tentatively suggest, eyeing some bottle his daughter had been prescribed for an ailment specifically feminine. It is dubious what its effect on him would have been; as it was he caused considerable embar-rassment, for such subjects were then taboo, and no doubt called forth a sharp retort from his daughter, Nel, a younger and as regards her father a less indulgent edition of Auntie.

My memories of Cousin Nel are more vivid than those I have of Auntie. She played an important part in our life for so long as we remained in Aberdeen. When I was small she alarmed me quite as much as did Auntie, but I soon came to know her better and I was proud when she showed approval of me. Yet in a way she too must have been a source of at least anxiety to her mother; for she was plain at a time when to justify her existence a woman must have at least looks enough "to secure herself a husband", and, what is more, a time when there were no "aids to beauty" and a girl must take as final what she saw in the mirror. I am not certain she was as plain as was taken for granted in the family. She was not indifferent to her appearance. She never let herself go at a time when women in far-off Scotland tended to "dress" only for occasions. She chose her clothes according to a system of her own which she called the "three colour system": two colours that blended were brought to life by a touch of a third more arresting. She had plenty of rich brown hair, but she wore it in a flat puff on top of her head as was then the custom, if not necessarily the fashion. She was high-complexioned from much fresh air and probably many cold baths, and I believe I never saw her but in a long bell-shaped skirt, separated from a shirt blouse with a whale-boned high collar by a stout leather belt, all of which tended to emphasise her forms while leaving her bosom a single undefined swell. What no doubt sealed her fate was that on a nose sharpened perhaps on her own wit (and she was very witty) sat a pince-nez looped to her ear by a fine gold chain. In spite of it all, hers was a pleasant face and one of the few from my childhood which I can still conjure up clearly. Its expression was firm almost to determination, but it was cheerful and humorous with not a discontented nor a drooping line upon it.

Cousin Nel taught in a private school for girls and she must have been an excellent teacher. She loved young people. She had an enthusiasm that was catching and a genius for making children useful in such a way as to make it seem a game. Like Auntie she had strict standards. They were not conventional ones. In a world of sleep-walkers she at least was awake, taking no one else's opinion on trust. When Alice and Letty came home from a few days' visit to the big house in Old Aberdeen, they told me how on the first evening when going to bed they had carefully folded their clothes on a chair to make a good impression, and how Cousin Nel, on coming upstairs to bid them goodnight, had cried: "Most unhealthy!" and flung the garments about the room to "air them". The ice was broken, but only up to a point. Cousin Nel knew her place and she knew ours.

I only once stayed with the Cowans (that was their name), and it was not in their Aberdeen house but one they had rented in Stonehaven for the Easter holidays. I went there with Letty. Cousin Nel took us in charge from the moment we arrived. She led us active lives which left us no time for our pet vices of dreaming and quarrelling. I remember that visit as a happy one. She often took us walks in the afternoon and they never bored us. She invented endless games to play as we went. They slipped my memory long, long ago, but somehow one of them got caught in the nets of time and a wave of association washed it to the surface when I began thinking of Cousin Nel. We played it in a wood whose ground was mapped for us in a rather curious way. A big house stood in the wood which we must never approach and which we knew as the Ogre's Castle. It was fraught with some mysterious danger. There were other danger zones besides, but with certain precautions we could venture onto them though we were warned that at Cousin Nel's cry of "Cavé!" we must take cover (having incidentally learned our first word of Latin). One of these spots was a clearing and what threatened us within its precincts was the Evil Eye. Another clearing was known as the Magic Circle and on it we were safe from danger of whatever sort.

The explanation of all this was given me years later when I was already in my sixties. I was staying with my sister Molly in Cambridge and our conversation turned to Cousin Nel, long dead. "And didn't you know?" asked Molly in amazement, "Didn't you know that the wood was a private park, the castle a private house and the ogre the owner?" No; I had not known, nor that the Evil Eye was the eye of the lurking game-keeper and the first clearing a place particularly exposed to it, while the second and safe one lay beyond the bounds of the property. In fact, when we played this exciting and enjoyable game with our respectable school-mistress cousin we were trespassing and liable, all three of us, if not to the prosecution that threatened the unwary from all "Private Property" notices in Scotland (though by Scotch Law trespassers are NOT liable to prosecution), then to final and humiliating banishment from the Ogre's grounds. Those were the days!

But to return to our Stonehaven visit: in the mornings Cousin Nel usually took Letty and me shopping, turn and turn about on the carrier of her bicycle. On these occasions she had a delightful habit of suddenly suggesting: "Shall we pick a bit?" and we soon learned this meant we were going to a tea-shop to eat cakes. She had a genius for leavening the even tenor of a useful active life with unexpected small pleasures. We might perhaps be sitting in the drawing-room on a quiet evening, each with her book and Auntie with her knitting, when Cousin Nel's eye would grow dreamy and she would lay her book aside, sigh, and in tones of resignation would murmur: "Man must live!" It was the signal for her to rise and fetch from some hiding-place a bag containing a mixture of caramels and chocolates which she handed round. Cakes and sweets play an important part in the lives of large families of sober upbringing, but even more were we appreciative of the gratuitous in life, the unexpected, and all this Cousin Nel knew intuitively through her love of young people.

Cousin Nel had a tragic end. I never knew the name of the disease that destroyed her. She discovered one day that she had lost the sensation of her feet and little by little she became paralysed. I never saw her during her long illness, for by that time we had moved to Edinburgh, but my mother told me that she kept her spirits to the end, never complaining but remarking on one occasion that the only thing to which she really objected was when people "who shall be nameless" came and prayed over her. She referred of course to her infinitely good but clumsy father.

I have very little to say about our fourth guest on Christmas Day; he played no great part in our Aberdeen life. Certainly for us children, living as we did in what was practically a gynaeceum, he had the prestige of being a man. But he was a small man, not at all handsome and inclined to be fat. On the whole we tended to take him as a joke. He proved, however, to have been more observant of us than we had been of him. When at his death he bequeathed a sum of money to Letty, by then married and living in New York, he achieved in my mind a sort of posthumous rehabilitation. For sheer gratuity – in the sense of unexpectedness – it was a gesture worthy of Cousin Nel.

These then were the guests who gathered round our dining-room table on Christmas Day to share the Christmas lunch after which we all trooped upstairs to the drawing-room for the Christmas-tree. It was lighted with real candles and hung with tangerines and walnuts wrapped in silver paper, besides the more conventional tinsel ornaments. The presents were heaped on the floor at the foot of the tree, a thing I always regretted because in picture-books toys are always attached to the tree, which seemed to set a standard we were not complying with.

For years my chief present was a doll. Letty and I had a second life we lived through our dolls. We had a third which we spun together in the form of an endless story while our Swiss governess of the moment was taking us for our daily walk. We were the heroines of our story, but we never identified with our dolls. They took their characters from people, children we happened to admire (and we had a rare gift for admiration), or they sprang to a life of their own we had recognised as latent the moment we saw them.

Up to the time of our learning to read for ourselves, and by that I mean read with pleasure, the thread that ran through our days was the poetry our father read aloud to us from our very beginnings, and the legends, fairy-tales and Bible stories our mother read to us when she came to say "good-night" to us in bed. When we did reach the stage of reading for ourselves, we came under a less fortunate influence; for the three of us, Alice, Letty and myself, were early seduced by the books of a certain Dorothea Moore, very popular at that time. We found in them a much more satisfactory version of the sort of stuff our daydreams were made of than anything we could invent for ourselves. These stories were all about little girls in whose background hovered the adult male without whom the book would have had no interest for us. The first that came our way was *My Lady Bellamy*, and it remained our favourite, though *Terry the Girl Guide*, the story of a more modern heroine, very nearly ousted it.

My Lady Bellamy was the story of a child of twelve recently married to a young Irish royalist, and promptly separated from him and sent to an aunt in England to have her education completed. He, in the meantime, was caught up in the royalist cause in defence of Charles the First of England. The book starts off with a dramatic scene in which Henrietta Bellamy saves her husband, who has suddenly appeared, breathless but gallant, over the wall of the garden where she is making a snowman, with the Roundheads hot on his heels. She works him into her snowman before the Roundheads discover his tracks, and from there she goes straight ahead with scarcely a setback till she has triumphed over his enemies, even the "cat-

eyed man". There were two volumes about Henrietta and her
Cavalier husband, but Letty and I lost interest when it came to
volume two because by then Henrietta had reached the bor-
ing age of eighteen, too old for us to identify with.

It is impossible to exaggerate the influence these books had
on our childhood. We were the more fascinated that Molly
had at some time been introduced to Dorothea Moore and
had, so the story ran, served as a model for Henrietta Bellamy.
We eventually all met the lady. We were taken to have tea
with her in the hotel where she was staying during a visit to
Aberdeen. I have only the vaguest memories of her as a very
feminine creature with a melting way about her. She was
eclipsed for us utterly by her brother, glorious in officer's uniform (it must have been early in the war) and romantically
Irish. In fact it was obvious even to us that here was the original of Sir Gervase Bellamy. It was natural that we should have
eyes only for him and he played his part to perfection, swing-
ing us off our feet and inventing games for us to play with
such verve that he left each of us feeling she had captured his
heart. By the time we left for home we were all in love with
him and Letty and I promptly gave him a new span of vicari-
ous life as the hero of the endless story we wove as we walked
the streets of Aberdeen.

None of this was fortunate in the peculiar circumstances of
our childhood. Women bounded our horizon on every side:
Mother, Swiss governess, Scotch Nanny, sisters but no brothers, maids in the kitchen, and innumerable aunts. There were
uncles too but we saw little of them. Man for us was represented by the master of the house, the genius who was always
at work and must never be disturbed but who would every
now and then irrupt into our lives by calling us down to join
him by the study fire with the magical words: "I'll read you
some poetry!"

For each of us in turn this poetry-reading began at an age when all we could grasp of it was its music; and I remember the shock it was to me when later I went to school and was asked to "render in my own words" a poem I knew by heart but only as intoxicating sound. It had never occurred to me that poetry could be turned into everyday speech; but I knew that for my father it was the very matter of life.

One occasion, one poetry-reading stands out as clear as clear in my memory. Our mother was out for the evening and Letty and I were already in bed and preparing to sleep when the call came. Tense with excitement we sprang out of bed, threw on our dressing-gowns and without even hunting for our bedroom slippers drew our long black woollen stockings halfway up our legs and stumbled down to join him, stocking-feet flapping in front of us. He read us Matthew Arnold's "Sohrab and Rustum" and for once he told us beforehand what the poem was about. As we settled down on cushions by the fire I remember a momentary fear lest our mother should return – who disapproved not of poetry but of late nights – but from the moment his voice rose on the first words we were under the spell and all else was forgotten. Like Yeats, my father read poetry as though the words were strung on a ribbon of sound. As in music the rhythm was fundamental, the rhythm, not the beat. I could tell through closed doors when it was poetry he was reading, and I can hear his voice still though he has been dead a quarter of a century. Compared to that passionate chant – it is the wrong word but there is none that fits, though "winged speech" comes nearest – ordinary speech sounded clipped and brittle, earth-bound, dead. When at last we heard the sound of our mother's return and escaped to bed, the waves danced in our heads and the new-born stars shone for us on the Aral Sea.

But I have lost my way in the frontierless fields of memory, where order is associative, not chronological. On the rifled tree the candles have burned out. Christmas Day is disintegrating. Several aunts and a few uncles have appeared and the balance has shifted in favour of the grown-ups. It is the frightening hour when fragile balloons are blown up by our intrepid elders till they burst, or are let fly to finish noisily on candle, fire or glowing pipe-bowl; the room is full of traps. I am the readier for bed that loud noises were always my terror, so up we go to a room made strange and deliciously disquieting by the shifting coal. Shadows loom menacingly till the fire flares briefly and familiar objects spring forward to reassure us, then sinks till only a redly glowing eye passively notes the invading darkness. Christmas Day is over.

CHAPTER TWO

Seven King's Gate

Seven King's Gate where we lived, father, mother and five daughters, was not an old house. I believe we were the first people to inhabit it, so it must have been built at the very beginning of the century. In the early days of their marriage my parents had lived in a fine old house which I only knew from a few dim photographs, and from hearing it so often spoken of. It stood in Old Aberdeen where a number of university professors lived, near King's College, one of the oldest and most beautiful universities in Britain, whose newly created chair of Rhetoric and English Literature my father was the first to hold. But when Alice, the third baby, was on her way, my mother's father, Alexander Ogston, Professor of Military Surgery and surgeon-in-ordinary to the Royal Family in Scotland, pronounced the house to be damp and advised my parents to move to the new part of the city. My grandfather's word was law, at least with my mother; but I think my father always regretted the change. He seemed to be a man who was oblivious to his surroundings, being always absorbed in his thoughts; but I well remember how suddenly he would spring free of them and see, and I know he was only at ease among objects of a certain beauty. I often heard him refer nostalgically to the "Don Street house" and I thought it fitting that he should have chanced to live in a street that bore the name, as I believed, of the poet he had, by his masterly editing of the original texts, restored to his full glory, and who in return had made my father's reputation as a scholar. The fact is that I mispronounced John Donne's name, as many people do.

The new house was a typical Aberdeen house, built of solid granite and allowing for the old-fashioned separation between parents, children and domestic staff. I realize now that it had not an atom of beauty (as a child I saw it with my heart, not with my eyes) but neither was it disfigured by any of the pretentious "Scottish baronial" excrescences which were then fashionable. Ours was a sober house, sober and solid.

I left Aberdeen when I was eleven, but Seven King's Gate dwells within me and I could explore it with the inner eye to this day, with perhaps a few gaps on the ground floor or semi-basement (the house was built on a slope). I clearly remember the huge laundry with its copper boiler and its long row of deep sinks in front of a window that opened onto the garden. A nightmare vision of my childhood was of sheep's heads soaking in blood-stained water in one of those sinks; in economical Scotland sheep's heads were then a recognized if not a popular dish. I remember, too, the ironing room and the red-hot cast-iron stove on which the irons were heated, the smell of singed cloth from the pads they were held with, the sizzle when one of the maids tested hers with a spittle-damp finger. A professional laundress in an enveloping white apron came on occasion to help with the ironing and she used no such amateur method but gauged her iron's degree of readiness by holding it close to her cheek. Then there was the wine-cellar, and another long narrow storeroom where I often watched my mother put eggs to preserve in a stone jar full of some appropriate liquid. She taught me to distinguish when an egg was imperceptibly cracked and unfit for preserving by the sound it made when lightly tapped against another egg; but I was to grow up into a world so different from my mother's that I was never required to preserve eggs.

So much for the ground floor, which communicated with the garden. If, on the other hand, you entered the house from the opposite side, by the front door which you reached through a small front garden and up a short flight of steps, then you found yourself in the adult world of responsibility and social intercourse. On the right as you passed through the hall was a small cloakroom where guests could hang their coats and wash their hands. Beyond was the staircase with its red "Turkey carpet" of which we were so proud. Under the staircase was my mother's private store-cupboard. It had a place in our family's mythology because Alice, the third of the family, was once tempted to taste the contents of a tin marked "Salts of Lemon" and dire results were expected. Nothing however happened, except a reaction to the emetic she was administered, but the incident served its purpose. I dared loot nothing, convinced that danger lurked in every tin and every paper bag.

On the left of the hall was my father's study, full of light from the two tall windows and big enough for the Chippendale dining-room table from his father's house in Shetland, on which he always wrote, to slip harmoniously into place on the opposite side to the fireplace. The dining-room was at the far end of the hall facing the front door, and its window overlooked the back garden. I sometimes spent an hour or so there with my mother in the morning, probably while my elder sisters were at school or doing their lessons in the schoolroom and the nurseries were being cleaned. On these occasions I often assisted at my mother's morning ritual with the butter and salt. By her standards, preserving eggs and renewing the butter-dishes and salt-cellars were, with jam making, the traditional tasks of the mistress of a house. She once told me you could judge a woman's value as a house-keeper by the look of her salt-cellars. It made a deep impression on me, and when I married and went to live in France, for a time I strove to live up to her standards. I soon discovered that salt-cellars have not the same significance in France where it is considered rather ill-bred to add salt to a dish, suggesting as it does some fault in the cooking. I was the only one to use my salt-cellars and I left off at last when an excellent cook we had at the time concluded that she was putting too little salt in her cooking and increased the dose daily till my husband complained.

Between the study and the dining-room a swing-door to the left led from the hall by way of a passage to the kitchen. When I was small this door was an object of terror to me because Molly, our eldest, had once pinched her thumb in it and "lost her nail". Beyond this door the passage passed first a pantry to the left, and to the left again the head of a steep staircase which dipped down to the back door and beyond to the cellars. At the end of the passage was the kitchen, which I remember as a large sunny room with primrose-coloured walls and a big window overlooking the back garden. A scullery and a larder opened off the kitchen on the side opposite the door. On the floor of the larder stood a row of great earthenware jars reminiscent of Ali Baba. As I remember things, one of them held oatmeal, one flour, and another brown "cooking" sugar which had a convenient way of form-ing into lumps easy to extract by hand.

We were not really supposed to pay visits to the kitchen, not from any notion that maids were unsuitable company for children, but because our mother knew that children can be troublesome in a kitchen and lead to "complaints from the cook", a thing she would have gone a long way to avoid. The interdiction only added to the charm the kitchen had for me,

largely on account of the larder, and I would seize any opportunity of lingering there, breathing in the smells: roasting
mutton, hot apple tart, steamed treacle pudding and newly
chopped parsley.

On the next floor the most important room was the
drawing-room, L-shaped and charming, with tall windows
and an intricate carved mantelpiece, convenient for hiding the
thimble when there was a children's party at home and we
played "Hunt the Thimble". It was a real drawing-room in
the sense that it had something ceremonious about it, a quality achieved because our mother had gathered there everything
she treasured and had done so with great good taste.
Ceremonious too because it was never marred by untidiness.
Yet it was neither artificial nor stilted nor in any way ostent-
atious, nor was it kept exclusively for visitors. Indeed, as I
remember things our mother usually sat there in the afternoon. After dinner she would join my father in the study,
unless he was correcting examination papers, a bad time for
everyone, and he would read her poetry while she did her
mending, a thing which, as he much later confessed to me,
distressed him considerably. Poetry needed all one's attention.
He had probably no notion how easily most women can concentrate their minds on something extraneous to what, on
their own responsibility, their hands are doing.

My mother had natural taste; fortunately, for unlike my
father, whose father's house in Shetland seems to have been
full of beautiful furniture, she had always lived in the atmosphere of solid ugliness that reigned in 252 Union Street, her
father's house. Always, except during one year. When she was
eighteen her father sent her to Copenhagen to study with a
Danish sculptor by name of Saabye, well known at the time,
and whose bust of her always stood in our drawing-room and
now stands in mine. Grandpapa did this partly to develop a

talent for drawing and painting he had noticed in her, and partly to give her some relief from the atmosphere of 252 Union Street and her strained relations with her step-mother. In Copenhagen she may well have developed an interest in furniture, and though it came as a shock to her when during their engagement my father went out and spent the greater part of the sum she counted upon to furnish the whole house, on a set of eighteenth-century feather-backed dining-room chairs, she was quick to recognize their beauty. By the time we went to live in Edinburgh she was buying on her own account and used to spend whole afternoons at the auction sales rooms. I grew up in a house full of lovely things, many of which came from the Griersons' house in Shetland, but many more she had picked up at these sales for some trifling sum and brought home in triumph.

On the same floor as the drawing-room, to its left, was my father's dressing-room. To the right a passage led to our parents' bathroom and bedroom. Parallel with the bathroom was a room where apples were stored and where hung my mother's rag-bag, full of fascinating odds and ends of material useful for dressing dolls. On the same floor, at the top of the stairs to the right, was a big spare bedroom in whose four-poster bed some famous poets and men of letters have slept; and where, when one of us children ran a temperature, she would be put in isolation till her ailment had been diagnosed, with beside her a rather lovely little French clock whose virtue was that, night or day, you had only to press a button for the coming hour to strike. If, however, some common childhood's illness was all the doctor diagnosed, then back we went to the night nursery on the principle that we might as well all have it together and get it over.

The top floor of the house was our domain. It consisted of a nursery, a night-nursery, a schoolroom, and a bedroom which Molly and Flora shared. There was also a pantry where, when we reached the age of relative reason, we were allowed to make toffee on the gas-ring, and a bathroom containing no fixed bath but only a tub. On winter evenings this tub would be carried through to the night-nursery and the three youngest of us would be given a bath before a glowing fire of good Scotch coal, and then rubbed dry with the towels old Nanny had put to warm on the fire-guard. It was one of the delightful memories of my very early childhood. Later we used all three to pile into our parents' bath, the most quick-witted having "bagged" the best end to sit in, the moment we were called to bed. All these rooms opened onto a square landing. A small gate at the head of the staircase cut us off from the grown-up part of the house.

Our other domain was the back garden. The small front garden was nearer in spirit to a shop window than a garden. Its purpose no doubt was to indicate that we were respectable order-loving people. The real garden was at the back of the house and in it each of us had a small plot of ground in which to sow seeds. A high wall sheltered us from curious eyes and all round at the foot of the walls were flower-beds. I remember especially two rose bushes (for some reason one belonged to Molly and the other to Flora; no doubt they had been brought from the Don Street garden); clumps of huge scarlet poppies whose buds we loved to force open to see the tightly folded crinkled petals inside, and which fascinated us by their association with sleep; a tea-rose that grew up the wall under the dining-room window and on which we were first taught to recognize and destroy suckers; and a low spreading plant with sweet-smelling leaves which we knew as Granny's Bedstraw.

In the middle of the garden was a long rough lawn where dandelions throve. It was built on two levels and joined by a grassy bank. At the far end of the garden grew a row of rowan-trees and beside them was our sand-pit. Near the house stood our swing. In fine weather we were oftener in the garden than in the house, but whatever the weather the tradition of our childhood required that in the afternoon we be taken for a walk.

The important figures in our nursery were our old Scotch Nanny already mentioned, and Jeannie Bisset, who came to help when I was still a baby, and took over from Nanny when she retired a couple of years later. In the schoolroom a series of Swiss governesses succeeded each other until the First World War sent the last of them home to her mountain fastness. On the outer circle hovered fat Miss Smith, known behind her back as Smithums, who gave each of us in turn our first lessons, Miss Cran who taught us to play the pianoforte, and a couple of bird-like little ladies to whom we went for sol-fa and singing lessons. There was also Miss Henry whose dancing lessons we attended, but none of these latter were important in our affections. Except for Miss Cran and Miss Henry, they all disappeared when we went to school.

Nanny was so old when I was born that when once my mother found her nodding over the fire with me on her knees she confided in our family doctor a fear that perhaps she was too old to be trusted with an infant. He laughed and assured her that a woman who has spent her life looking after babies will never, not even in her sleep, let one of her charges fall into the fire. And so Nanny remained to fix in my young mind a clear image of the impersonal, maternal benevolence she embodied, though she herself had never borne a child. I loved her as dearly as I loved my mother but it was a love of a different sort and free of the anguished fear of death that haunted my feeling for my mother, and which again and again she would laughingly pluck like a thorn from my heart, saying she came of a long-lived family, and quoting an old cousin of her father's who when she reached the age of ninety had assured her that "the best of life is over at eighty". That gave me time.

I am not certain what age I was when Jeannie Bisset first came to second Nanny in the nursery, but my earliest memory of all is of the first time she accompanied us when Nanny took me for my afternoon outing in the perambulator. At first Nanny wheeled me, but every now and then she would tentatively hand me over to Jeannie, hoping to accustom me to her presence. Every time I howled. Yet I know perfectly well, and I know it because I remember it, that my howling was a matter of principle. I took to Jeannie from the first moment I saw her, but I was accustomed to being wheeled by Nanny and already custom was sacred. By the time Nanny retired Jeannie shared her place in my heart, and hers is, with Cousin Nel's, one of the few faces from my childhood which I remember clearly, and even now it brings with it a feeling of peace, confidence and security.

The Swiss governesses were at first shadow figures. Their business was with Molly and Flora, though they took enough interest in the rest of us to allow us to acquire French almost as early as English.

My mother maintained that in my case French and English came simultaneously. The first Swiss governess I remember was Mademoiselle Gagnebin, but only as a gentle well-bred presence, loved by all. I remember more clearly her successor, Mademoiselle Jacques. Her sister was governess to the children of Sir George Adam Smith, then Principal of Aberdeen University, and the general impression was that they had got the best of the bargain. Our Mademoiselle Jacques was a strange silent creature with a sallow complexion and a sulky face who had no real interest in children. I have a curious

memory of the evening she had the epileptic fit which probably accounted for her strangeness and brought her time with
us to an end. We were in the cottage on our grandfather's
estate near Dinnet where we used to spend our summers. Our
parents had gone to dine at Glendavan, our grandfather's
house, and Mademoiselle was sitting on the window seat in
the nursery, reading us our bedtime story in French when the
fit seized her. She suddenly began to stutter over the word
"minute" and rose to her feet, still struggling to say it. The
next thing she was lying on the floor, twitching. Alice
shrieked for the maids and there was a great deal of excitement while everyone gathered round giving advice, and Letty
and I remained round-eyed in our beds. Then someone ran
off to fetch our parents from their dinner-party, and perhaps
Grandpapa, as a doctor. I remember nothing more.

Mademoiselle Jacques was succeeded by Mademoiselle
Schoepfer (it sounds like the kings of England). She was my
favourite and the one I came to know best. She used to take
us for long walks, robbing them of their boredom by teaching
us to sing part-songs whose rhythm telescoped the miles we
covered. When we were at Dinnet she gave these walks purpose by setting us to hunt for and gather raspberries and
mushrooms as a surprise for our Mother; and when my sisters'
teasing reduced me to tears, as happened often, she would
comfort me by singing:

> "*Ne pleure pas Jeannette,*
> *Tra la-la-la-la-la-la-la,*
> *Ne pleure pas Jeannette*
> *On te mariera on te mar-i-er-a!*"

– thereby opening up to me vistas of escape. Much later she
herself married and settled in Geneva where I saw her again
when I became engaged to the French grandson of a Geneva

banker. She was delighted that my French should have proved so useful, and I that her song should have been so prophetic.

I have an odd memory in connection with Mademoiselle Schoepfer. She once took me to a part of Aberdeen where I had never been. We were in search of an address she had on a slip of paper. It had been given her by a Dutchman she had met somewhere, perhaps during her journey from Geneva to Aberdeen. She wanted to see what sort of place he lived in. Our search took us to what seemed to us both a rather disreputable part of the city. For years I remembered the name of the street and I still remember the name of the Dutchman, which was Pfeiffer. We agreed to go no farther, and as we hastened home she gave me strict injunctions as to silence and secrecy. I have kept her innocent secret till today.

CHAPTER THREE

The Grierson Girls

The people mentioned in the last chapter were the props on which the everyday fabric of our life reposed. Equally important were certain recurrent occasions and ceremonies which gave it shape and substance. Next to Christmas in importance were the children's parties. Even our birthdays were lesser events. I think our mother disapproved of the principle of birthday parties, implying as it seems to do a request for a present. Besides which, she could never have faced five birthday parties of which three fell in January, without counting our father, also a January child.

The ceremony for each of us consisted in a tray, bearing our presents, brought to us on waking, a luncheon of our own choosing, and at tea-time the birthday cake with candles and crackers. Actually I am not quite certain about the crackers. I am perhaps embroidering on the familiar theme. However that may be, the children's parties, of which there were a number every winter, roused greater excitement, aggravated rather than attenuated by the precautions that were taken to keep us calm. We were sent to lie down in the early afternoon, with blinds and curtains drawn, but the air vibrated with our expectancy. Old Nanny did her best to quiet our whispered conversations. She must have succeeded because I can remember my amazement when I woke to find that I had slept.

The next thing was to dress us. I cared about my appearance from the start and clothes early posed me the problem of how to combine becomingness with comfort. My mother added to my distress and complicated the situation by insisting also on warmth. Every autumn there were terrible scenes when the time came to put me into what were known as "combinations", perhaps because they combined warmth with discomfort. They had long sleeves and close-fitting legs and, as I remember it, were not made of the softest wool. I have always hated close-fitting garments and in these combinations I felt so held-in I could think of nothing else. On the first chill autumn morning when they were brought out, smelling of moth-ball, from their summer storage, I would scream and struggle while about me mother and nurse alternately coaxed and threatened. In the end I had to give in, as sooner or later children must.

When it came to dressing for a party no concession was made, except that party combinations were short-sleeved. Over them were put, one by one, our party clothes: a small flannel bodice to fix our stockings to, a flannel petticoat, a starched, open-work cotton petticoat, and at last, invariably, a white embroidered muslin party dress. On our legs we wore fine black open-work mercerized cotton stockings and bronze dancing pumps. Yes; but for the drive were added black, woollen stockings and the sort of snow boots I associated with Uncle Henry. Our five heads of hair had by now been brushed till they gleamed and drawn back unbecomingly under black velvet "snoods". When all this was done we were wrapped up in Shetland shawls and hurried down to the patiently waiting cab.

The parties to which we were invited often took place in the houses of university colleagues of our father, in Old Aberdeen. It was a long slow journey in the horse-cab, which our mother preferred to the new taxicabs, because it had no meter to tick up the price while she struggled to get me dressed; a long, slow journey, sometimes over a light powdering of snow, but it had for us the charm of an orchestra tuning up. Once in the drawing-room where the party took place I soon forgot my combinations and gave myself up to enjoyment. There would be a roaring fire in the hearth (central heating was unheard of in Scotland in those days, or, if heard of, disapproved of), an after-Christmas smell of candles, and the prospect of a delicious supper. There would sometimes be electricity in the house we were visiting and we would invent excuses to escape to the passages and staircase to try the switches. Electricity was still a novelty in Scotland at the time and only to be found in the houses of the rich and important, or in hotels; and the part it played in our childhood was out of all proportion to its indubitable advantages. Indeed, electricity had come to symbolize for us a whole way of life, a social status, an emancipation. Its absence humiliated us. In the early stages of a new friendship I would even try to conceal this lack, though the probability was that the little girl I was striving to deceive was no better off than myself in this respect. Letty and I would even try to conceal it from complete strangers whose faces we would never see; for we had discovered that if you turned the "incandescent" type of gas bracket off and then quickly on again before the mantle had time to cool, then it lighted again. We often did so, hoping the passers-by in the street below would see the light flash off and on and infer that we had electricity.

Among the houses favoured with electricity where our parties took place, the one I best remember is Chanonry Lodge, the official residence of the Principal of the University, the Sir George Adam Smith already referred to, and I do believe that a certain reticence towards his children in those early years stemmed from our jealousy that they should have reached such heights when we must still fumble for matches by the light of a street lamp shining through the window before we could dispel our ghosts. And of course, there was the matter of the Swiss governess. But that reticence had another source to which I am coming.

The games we played at all these parties were the old familiar games, with one dreaded exception. Nuts in May, Oranges and Lemons, Hunt the Thimble and Hide and Seek we could all enjoy; but the Adam Smiths, whose family included a number of lively, self-confident boys, had inaugurated a new game called "Tomahawk", and I remember with what dread I used to glance to right and to left as we entered their drawing-room to ascertain whether or not a tomahawk had been prepared and put to wait its hour in some quiet corner. It was always there, looking innocent enough to the uninitiate, a mere club made by rolling newspapers tightly together to form a thick stick, the whole consolidated with string.

The game was usually the last to be played, but the certainty of its coming took, for me, the bloom off the party. When the time came we were all made to sit in a ring while one of the children, usually, as I remember things, a very excited Adam Smith boy, took up his position in the centre, grasping the tomahawk. His business was to hit one of the waiting, apprehensive children and then throw the tomahawk down and rush back to his stool. The child he hit must pick it up and hit him back before he got there. If he failed then he took his turn with the tomahawk. Or was it if he succeeded? I forget. I used whenever possible to make my escape the moment joyful Adam Smith voices began crying out for a game of tomahawk. On one occasion I crept upstairs to a bedroom and fell asleep on the bed. I was later roused by the sound of laughter.

Kathleen, the most self-possessed of the Adam Smith girls, had found me out.

I believe there was a story current in Aberdeen according to which when the Grierson girls went to a party they played among themselves, forming an exclusive phalanx. It is quite certainly a myth and no doubt had its roots in the game of Tomahawk. What is more, it is contradicted by a story of my mother's, who later told me how hurt she had been when, at the end of a party, the mother of other children remarked to her: "Yours are plain little things, but they can talk!"

Of all the parties, the best were those given in celebration of Hallowe'en. An appropriate atmosphere was created by the classic method of lighting candles in turnips hollowed out to resemble death's heads. The games we played were well-known to everyone: ducking for apples in a tub of water (you had to grasp them with your teeth); or with greater skill and less embarrassment striving to spear an apple by dropping a carefully aimed fork; or catching apples suspended from a string, again with one's teeth unaided by the hands. The apples we won we carried home as proof of our skill. I believe it was at the Hallowe'en parties that we played another game which I loved to watch but feared to join in. The lights would be put out and a large dish of sultanas steeped in brandy set alight. The object of the game was to snatch handfuls of the sultanas from out of the blue flames which rose terrifyingly from the silver platter containing them. In vain my mother assured me that burning brandy does not hurt because it goes out at once. I lacked the courage to try though I longed to eat the sultanas.

More secretly, at home we would throw over our shoulder the skin of an apple, peeled without a break, and strive to decipher the initial it formed on falling, the initial of our future true love.

Close on the heels of the children's parties came other occasions of a festive nature which were as much a part of our life's pattern as they were. Every spring our mother planned an excursion to Muchalls by the sea, to gather the first primroses, or to Dunnottar where the ruins of a medieval castle fired our imaginations, or to the lighthouse at the mouth of the Don. These excursions involved a short train journey and picnic-baskets. The uncertain Scotch climate added an element of tension to the general excitement all such outings roused in us. We would wake and listen fearfully for rain. If we heard its patter on the leaves outside we would comfort ourselves by quoting a local saying, "Rain before seven, dry before eleven", and often it was justified.

On Easter Day when the weather was fine we would sally out to the woods outside Aberdeen with our tea-basket, and our mother would hide coloured eggs and marzipan effigies of the Easter Hare for us to hunt for. Once every spring we were invited to the house of Sir James Bailey, one of the University professors, to gather daffodils in his park. He lived outside Aberdeen, and there was one tragic occasion when the cab that conveyed us had to turn back because a fall of late snow had blocked the road. Letty and I howled all the way home, such pleasure children take in celebrating each phase of the calendar as the year revolves.

Another of the great delights was sea-bathing. We must have been hardy children to take pleasure in that cruel sea with its biting cold and its rough waves. Here again it was the ceremony of the thing that was half the joy. We would set out with our Swiss governess on top of the tramcar, swaying along between the alternate pink and white hawthorn-trees that bordered one of the streets we followed. I remember trying to catch one of the branches as we passed and being told I might break my arm.

Those were the days of bathing-machines. How many people remember them? A bathing-machine was a wooden cabin mounted on high wheels to which a horse was harnessed when you were ready to go down to the sea. It left you at a point where you had only to descend a few wooden steps to find yourself over knee-deep in icy water. Inside them everything was sticky with salt water and when I stripped off my black woollen stockings I could feel underfoot the rough wet sand left by the last bather. When at last, with a rattle of chains, the horse was harnessed and set off on its jolting run down to the sea, I would shout out loud for very joy and excitement.

We were only allowed to stay ten minutes in the water (can we really have wanted to stay in longer?) and the moment we emerged from our battle with the waves we were rubbed dry and dressed and sent to run races on the sand to restore our circulation. Our furious appetites were then appeased with biscuits bought in packets from an open-air stall. Togo biscuits, they were called, in honour of the Japanese admiral who beat - can it have been the Russians? The Japanese were then our friends and allies, a delightful people, apt at making dolls in their own charming image. Or we would buy boiled cockles and eat them with the help of a pin. Sometimes we were allowed a sixpenny ride on the mouldy dromedary that went its slow proud way to and fro along the beach, led by its drab keeper. The rest of the afternoon we spent building sand castles, and that is one of the things that afforded me the deepest feeling of satisfaction ever experienced in childhood.

CHAPTER FOUR

Our Aberdeen Family

In Chapter One I told of the people who were with us on Christmas Day. They were all members of my mother's family, the Ogstons. The Grierson family descended from a clergyman who bought land in the Shetland Isles towards the end of the seventeenth century. Our father always insisted that he knew nothing of our branch of the Griersons before that time, and when Uncle Jimmie had a family tree drawn up where such things are done, and it traced us back to a Duke of Burgundy, his eye grew sceptical and he lost interest. I never saw that tree.

On his homeward journey this first ancestor lost his life when his ship foundered in a storm in the Pentland Firth. The deed of sale must have remained behind in Shetland, for this property, Quendale, became the centre from which the Grierson family came and went for some two hundred and fifty years, by which time all the members had died or scattered. These Shetland relatives were undoubtedly the most important to us children of all our relations, in the sense that by sheer force of personality they stood highest in our scale of values, rivalled only by our maternal grandfather, Alexander Ogston; but our Aberdeen family played a larger part in our early lives by being present among us, so I shall continue with them.

The above-mentioned Alexander Ogston married twice. It was his first wife, Mary Jane or Molly Hargrave, who was our grandmother, though we never met her. She came, on her mother's side, of an old Highland family, the Clan MacTavish of which her father, Dugald MacTavish, was Chieftain until poverty forced him to resign and earn his living in the Edinburgh Law Courts, a thing that broke his heart and ruined his temper. The MacTavishes had a long connection with the Hudson Bay Company, but it was not this connection that accounted directly for Molly Hargrave's having been born and brought up in Canada, as was the case. It was because her MacTavish mother had married a certain James Hargrave of more modest descent, whose parents had emigrated to Canada, and who had chanced to enter the service of the Hudson Bay Company. He had worked his way up to become Chief Factor of York Factory, one of the Company's fur-trading centres, and having done so had taken advantage of his net furlough to come back to Scotland in search of a wife. It was probably through a MacTavish son who was also at York Factory that he had an introduction to Dugald MacTavish and his family. He called there and fell in love with Letitia, one of the daughters.

One of my childhood memories is of the trunk full of old letters written home by our mother's forebears in the early dangerous days of trapping. She made copies of some of the most interesting of those letters but eventually gave them all to, I believe, the Canadian government because she was afraid we would none of us take an interest in them, in which she may have been wrong. When we were children she used to fascinate us with the story of how her mother, Molly Hargrave, had at the age of five been carried off by Red Indians. When she was found missing, search parties were sent off in every direction. It was her own father's party that found her in a Red Indian camp. The Chief explained that he had no intention of keeping her but had wanted to show her hair to his wives. She apparently had the glorious auburn hair which Aunt Flora, our mother's only real sister, inherited.

The other story about our grandmother is that she was brought to Scotland shortly after her father's death (her mother had died when she was six years old) by her step-mother, by all accounts an exceptional woman and, to judge by a daguerreotype taken in her middle age, a delightful person. The reason for this journey was that Molly had fallen in love with one of her suitors and her stepmother disapproved strongly of her choice. She was accordingly embarked on the sailing ship that tacked its slow way between Canada and Scotland. She had scarcely been a week in Aberdeen when she met my grandfather at a ball. He was already a brilliant young doctor and was so good-looking he came to be known as the "Adonis of the profession". They were soon engaged and soon married.

Six children were born of this marriage but only four survived, my mother, Uncle Hargrave, Aunt Flora and Uncle Walter. I know little of the facts of my grandmother's death. She left behind her an aura of youth, gaiety and charm which long outlived her. It may well be that Scotch Presbyterianism, which, as I knew it, readily took the form of respectability and a tendency to judge rather than love one's neighbour, proved to be too much for her free spirit. Certainly she had too many children in too short a time, and a husband too much involved in the research he strove to combine with earning a living for his growing family as a general practitioner to realize how far things had gone amiss. Moreover, like so many Scots, he had begun on occasion to drink too much, no doubt to wrest the maximum from such moments of joy and fellowship as came his way; for why else do we Scots drink, when drink we do?

Between our lowering skies and the bedrock of tragedy that underlies our national subconscious we need help before we can soar.

However that may be, he failed to take seriously the loss of spirits and the depression that wore her down during and after her last pregnancy, when she would sit listless in her room with the blinds drawn, dreaming perhaps of Canada. Before leaving the house he would come in and raise the blinds, telling her it was bad for her to sit in the dark; but as soon as he was gone she would draw them down again.

It took some time and a good deal of piecing together of scraps of information before I could face the fact that this grandmother of mine committed suicide with the help of some drug from her husband's laboratory.

None of this formed a part of my memory, but I was told of her early death when I was still a child, and how Grandpapa sat all night by her bedside. Later I was told how he made a vow, not never to drink again, as lesser spirits might have done, but never again to drink too much, and that he kept his vow. He never got over her death, so my mother told me, and at long last, before he himself died in his eighties, he asked to be buried beside her, leaving his second wife to her lonely grave.

For there was a second wife, as I said earlier. She was a woman we none of us loved. The story is that she trapped Alec Ogston into marriage by feigning an interest in his children which she only felt for himself. I was told that on returning from a journey he found her in his nursery with the four children gathered round her. She folded her arms about them and gazing appealingly at their father said: "Oh Alec, you can't send me away!" As she was in her cold way a beautiful young woman, and as his children badly (so he was told) needed a mother, he did not send her away in the sense she intended. But my mother once told me of a marriage her father nearly made at an earlier date, and of her retrospective regret that nothing should have come of it. He had had on one of his campaigns a young German baroness working under him as a voluntary nurse. They fell in love with each other and decided to marry, but for some reason there was a delay and Grandpapa returned to Scotland. They corresponded and in one of his letters Grandpapa, haunted perhaps by the memory of his first wife's tragedy, described our Scotch Sundays to his promised bride and said he was afraid she would find Aberdeen difficult to bear. She wrote back a troubled letter saying that obviously he no longer loved her and was inventing excuses to put her off. The iron man was so offended he ceased writing to her altogether and the whole thing came to nothing.

I shall return later to Grandpapa and his children by his first wife. At this point I shall only speak of his second batch of children. The eldest was Uncle Alfred, a very good-looking man with an impressive nose who was in the Consular Service and spent most of his time abroad. He married a first time and had a little girl, our cousin Esmée. He was consul in Messina at the time of the great earthquake and only just saved his own and his baby's life by taking refuge under the dining-room table. His wife, our aunt Ethel, who was in bed upstairs, was killed.

One of my earliest memories is connected with Aunt Ethel and Esmée. I must have been very young indeed at the time, so young that my mother at first refused to believe I wasn't inventing; but when I described to her how I had been taken out to the Langcroft garden and lifted to see my little cousin in her perambulator and could specify that it was green with a white mosquito-net in front of the hood, which was drawn aside to allow me to see the baby, she admitted that my facts were correct and that I had no other means of knowing them.

Esmée, who grew up to become a very pretty girl and a fine woman, was the bane of our early years. She was already an exceptionally pretty child and she now became the immediate concern of our Ogston aunts, who fussed round her like clucking hens. She was motherless, she was delicate, she was an only child. Not for her the rough life and plain food that were good enough for the five healthy Grierson girls. She must join in no exciting games, she must be protected against the sun by a sunshade and white gloves, and while we squeezed into the cottage, Langcroft, lent us by our grand-father, she spent her summer up at the "big house", the centre of grown-up attention, though probably not of Grandpapa's, and with free access to the uncles we all adored and would have liked to see more of. I liked Esmée not at all. And I envied her. I would have liked to be delicate, though I could not bring myself to want to be motherless. In fact, and as far as possible, I avoided her, while at the same time resenting that so little attempt should be made by our aunts to court our society for this fragile cousin. I knew it could only mean that they thought us too rough to be trusted with her.

Some years later, when he was posted in the United States, Uncle Alfred married again. His second wife was an American and I think he had two daughters by her. As he died without our ever seeing him again we never met any of them, but when after the long separation of the last war I met Esmée again, in Flora's house in Woodstock, she told me how dearly she had loved her American stepmother.

Next to Uncle Alfred came Aunt Helen, a radiantly beauti-ful creature with dark eyes and dark curly hair and a lovely speaking voice. As a young girl she had briefly joined the suffragettes and there is a story that she was once given the task of interrupting a meeting held by Lloyd George. She did so quite simply by calling out over the heads of the audience: "Mister Lloyd George!" every time he opened his mouth, and her low resonant voice made of the words a clarion call. A policeman hastened to eject her but she turned on him with the dog-whip she had hidden under her coat. She was nonetheless hauled off to the nearest police station. The legend is that the next morning's post brought her nine (or was it eleven?) offers of marriage, all of them from gentlemen unknown.

The man she actually married was not one of them. He was a London doctor who delighted our adolescence because he brought a breath of the World into our sober lives. Uncle Todd, we called him, I forget why. It was not his name. He flirted with us delightfully and took us rowing on the lake by moonlight, singing as he rowed the famous aria from *I Pagliacci*, with full tenor voice and carefully inserted sob. I think he must have been hideously bored during the summers he spent at Glendavan, and that his mild flirtations with us were his one relief, apart from the bridge table Grandpapa sometimes got together in the evening. He it was that sowed in our hearts the first seeds of discontent. We had never wanted to go anywhere but to our Grandfather's place in Aberdeenshire for our summer holidays. Uncle Todd now began telling us that we were being wasted in "this hole" and that if our parents had any sense of their responsibilities we would all be taken to do the season at Knokke. I remember the sudden fever that seized me, fear that perhaps he was right and that unless our parents did something active we might never meet any promising young men to marry. I must have been ten or eleven at the time.

Next to Aunt Helen, if I remember rightly, came Aunt Con, or Constance. She later changed her name to Renée and we had difficulty in making the changeover. She was a much duller person than Aunt Helen. Moreover she it was that took most interest in Esmée and so played no great part in our lives. After her came Uncle Axel, Aunt Rosa and Uncle Rannald, who was only nine years older than Molly and might have been the elder brother Letty and I so longed to possess. Aunt Rosa was next to Aunt Flora in my affections. She was the youngest of the aunts, blessed with a happy disposition and gifted in all the outdoor sports. I was more at ease with her than with Aunt Flora whose slightly caustic sense of humour was sometimes more than I could cope with in my early years.

Both Uncle Axel and Uncle Rannald were mobilised during the first World War. Both survived, but Uncle Axel died of the Spanish influenza before even he reached home. Uncle Rannald married and, as far as I was concerned, disappeared into London.

CHAPTER FIVE

Our Shetland Relatives

As I suggested earlier, our Shetland relatives were very different from our Aberdeenshire ones. Our mother used to tell us how shocked she was the first time she visited her family-in-law and heard their private affairs being freely discussed "in front of the servants". The Griersons' relationship with their domestic staff was feudal rather than middle-class. What is more, they enjoyed talking far too much to be careful what they said in front of anyone. There were six brothers and sisters in all, Uncle Jimmie, Aunt Lucy, my father, Aunt Lizzie, Uncle Barney (Bernard) and Uncle Andrew. Uncle Barney emigrated to Canada and Uncle Andrew died in India while still a young man so I never met either of them. We saw little of Aunt Lucy, but she was in some curious way important to us. She was probably the one that most resembled my father, very intelligent and lively. I remember her as a woman not in any way pretty but having a fine intelligent face, a little ravaged and ironical, and a general look of elegance. She had her legend, an intangible and elusive legend whose perfume was all that filtered through to us children. We sensed rather than knew that our mother's heart stood still when someone suggested that Flora "had a look of Lucy". We knew too that it had been "Lucy's latest" that the Griersons had discussed in a manner so unseemly "in front of the servants".

Beyond the fact of her being the object of considerable

anxiety, all I knew of her, in the sense of its forming a part of my memory, is that she did beautiful embroidery and that at some stage she became a Catholic. As regards the first, I once picked up a teacloth from a pile of clean linen my mother was putting away, and spread it out to admire its lovely design of flowers and leaves and winding stalks, all done in blues and reds with touches of yellow. My mother said: "Your Aunt Lucy embroidered it". I asked if I might keep it. I have it to this day, threadbare but still beautiful. As regards her Catholicism, a very early memory raises to the level of reality what otherwise would have been a part of family legend. I have a vivid flash-memory of going to one of the Aberdeen parks in a group of grown-ups one of whom was Aunt Lucy and another an old priest in flowing black robes, about whom there hung an aura of respect which mingles in memory with an inexplicable sense of malaise. No doubt the other grown-ups found so Catholic a man of God something of an embarrassment in an Aberdeen public garden.

I suppose the truth is that Aunt Lucy was wasted, as were so many women in those days, who were given no outlet for their gifts. She died somewhere in South America where she had gone as governess to some family. We were still children at the time.

Uncle Jimmie was, with Aunt Flora, the most important character in our childhood, and Aunt Lizzie and her husband, William Bruce, those that ultimately meant most to us. Uncle Jimmie provided the element of the unexpected that was lacking in our orderly lives. He would suddenly turn up and settle into our spare bedroom for an unspecified period of time, depending on his whim and the next boat to Shetland. I still have a vision of him lying behind a vast newspaper in the big four-poster bed, and hastily restoring his false teeth, when we burst in to bid him good-morning. He was so popular with us we could scarcely be made to wait till he was ready for us. His charm was immense and owed nothing to his looks, for beside the fact of his false teeth he was nearly bald and he was stout. It was a matter of sheer zest for life and the desire to please. It was as potent with women as with children. Certainly for us he was the sun that rose, the extra day in the leap-year, the exception that proves the rule. In short, he was the lightning that from time to time and always unexpectedly struck our tranquil lives and set them alight.

Wherever Uncle Jimmie took us, whether to the cinema, the theatre, a tea-room or down to the harbour, we were certain to be rushed there in a taxi-cab. Taxis were rare in our life in those early days because, as I said before, of their nasty habit of ticking the price up while the family assembled or we were made ready. Uncle Jimmie was, I believe, in continual financial difficulties, but they had no hampering effect on his sense of enjoyment. He had very little patience with my parents' sober habits and I remember him once remarking, to my great consternation, that if he had our father's income he would keep a motorcar. The truth is that the Griersons' Irish blood ran strong in his veins and he had the Irish way of missing an essential link in the chain of his logic. I was told that if he succeeded in restraining his impulse to buy some costly item he would then feel free to squander the sum he had "saved" on something equivalent.

Clearly I remember the occasion when he carried us off to a tea-room and offered a prize to the one that ate most cakes. Molly won. She ate eleven cakes while I worked my way through five and came in last. On the day of his departure he would taxi us down to the harbour and show us round the docks. Ships were his real world and there was not a cockle-shell he could not sail on any sea; so my father told me. When once as a young man the latter went to pay a visit of condolence to a crofter's wife whose son had been drowned out fishing, she said to him: "Oh Mr. Grierson, if your brother Jimmie had been with him his boat wouldn't have foundered". My father, who had left the islands for the city was "Mr. Grierson", but Uncle Jimmie was "Jimmie".

I never stayed at Uncle Jimmie's place in Shetland, Helendale. I never went to Shetland at all till after I was married and then it was to stay with Aunt Lizzie and Uncle William at Symbister. By that time Uncle Jimmie was dead and his place sold. But Molly has often told me how life there was lived when she and Flora went to stay. When they arrived they went up to the attic floor to choose their bedroom. They were then told they were free to do as they liked on two conditions: if any damage was done in the course of a game, such as breaking a window with a cricket-ball, then that game must be suspended till the following day; and they must be washed, brushed and changed when the dinner-gong sounded in the evening. There seem to have been no restrictions on lying in bed late. When they did come down they were certain to find coffee and tea, and on a sideboard covered dishes of several sorts. Uncle Jimmie himself ate a colossal breakfast, or so Molly said, eating of all the dishes and as often as not ringing for the maid at the end to announce to her: "I think I shall just top off with a couple of lightly boiled eggs".

Uncle William used to delight us with stories of Uncle Jimmie's youth. The one that most neatly captures the mixture of lordly bluff and lucid honesty which was a part of the latter's charm occurred when he was once showing an English guest – probably a member of his wife's family – round the premises. As they went from house to grounds Uncle Jimmie sensed that from his guest's point of view Helendale was no such great matter. So, with a wide gesture, he carelessly remarked: "Of course, I'm going to throw out a wing hereabouts to house the billiard-room, and I'm planning to expand the stables", then, at the first convenient opportunity he turned to where Uncle William followed, a silent tomb of laughter, and whispered: "If I could lay my hand on a five pound note I'd be thankful!"

Aunt Lizzie had a great deal of Uncle Jimmie's zest for life, but she had something else which was lacking in her brother, though looking back I can scarcely admit he had a fault, and which Aunt Lizzie probably owed to the influence of the man she married: a sense of responsibility. She took upon herself many of the tasks which should normally be the doctor's, but few doctors at the time were willing to bury themselves on those windswept islands. The crofters found it natural to bring their ailments to her, even when there was a doctor, and she found it as natural to devote her time to them. She regularly wrote my mother the liveliest accounts of life on Whalsay, the island they lived on, in an almost illegible hand. I remember one letter in which she described her Christmas Day. In the middle of stuffing the goose for luncheon she was called out to give first aid to a boy with a severed artery. There were also vivid accounts of the visits in the summer of the Admiral of the North Sea Fleet to Scapa Flow, and of outings in the Admiral's yacht. As my mother used to say, Aunt Lizzie gave one the impression that Whalsay was "the hub of the universe", yet a lonelier island it is hard to imagine. It was Aunt Lizzie's and Uncle William's gift for ceremony that gave life shape and meaning, and in this they had a close affinity with my mother. At Symbister there was no question of coming down late for breakfast. You must be ready when the bell sounded, as you must for every other meal. A housemaid brought you hot water in a large jug and prepared the tub in your room (what was known as a "sitz-bath") every evening before dinner, for bathroom there was none on Whalsay

Island; and as at Uncle Jimmie's you must appear neat and changed for dinner. On a certain day every autumn Aunt Lizzie and Uncle William changed their quarters to rooms more sheltered from the winter gales. On a certain day each spring they moved back to their summer quarters. Without this ceremony, without the deep interest they both took in the islanders, life in the long winter months would have been so empty there would have been little inducement to leave their beds in the morning. They solved in their own way the problem that drove so many to drink, and so many more to leave the islands and seek a livelihood elsewhere.

To the end Aunt Lizzie's greatest boast was to have preserved her husband's love unaltered. I remember her once saying to the three youngest of us: "My dears, it is something to have reached the age of sixty and to know that in your husband's eyes you are still just IT!" Yet she also told us that she had great difficulty in making up her mind when Uncle William made his offer of marriage. Her lively round eyes sparkled as she told us how she had wondered how she would bear to sit at breakfast every morning opposite "that seal's head!"

Seal's head or no, William Bruce of Symbister was one of the most attractive men I have known. He was an aristocrat in the truest sense of the word, needing no visible material signs of his inner worth. He could wear the oldest clothes and ride on a cart of hay without losing a whit of his inborn distinction. Aunt Lizzie once told me how, when he took her for the first time to visit the tombs of his ancestors in the family chapel (if I understood her rightly), she had "felt like a mushroom!" But there was more to Uncle William than his family tombs. Actually his story was that the first of his forebears to settle in Shetland had been a cousin of Robert the Bruce who had been exiled from Court for manslaughter. By the time the land descended to our Uncle there was no money left at all and he was as poor as a church mouse, depending on his rents which poverty forced him to collect for himself. He was Justice of the Peace for the region, but it is a servitude which brings in no remuneration. Gladstone's Crofters' Act ruined the Bruces, for though no doubt an excellent thing seen from one end of the telescope, the other view showed landlords with heavy obligations and uncertain rents. One of Uncle William's great grievances was that he had once had to supply the Manse's lavatory with a mahogany seat while he himself had but plain deal on the earth-closet which was housed in the romantic-looking little tower of Symbister House. When later summoned to pay a tax on the arms over the house-door he did, however, balk, telling them to remove them and be damned.

I do not know whether his strong objection to church and clergy came from the lavatory-seat incident, but I do know that he had such an objection, though he never imposed it on others.

Uncle William and his brother, Bertie, spoke with exactly the same intonation as "Lord HawHaw", the English traitor (or was he Irish?) who spoke from Germany to the British public during the last war. I was in German-occupied France at the time, and to hear the familiar voice prophesying the downfall of Britain was as good as any music-hall comedy, because if ever there was a pair of diehard Conservatives it was Uncle William and Uncle Bertie. The thrice repeated "Germany calling!" with twice a lift of the voice on the last syllable, and a drop the third time, was pure Uncle Bertie, who tended to be facetious, which Uncle William never was. His humour was laconic, for he was a man of few words. I remember my father getting worked up over some point, probably political, on which he and Uncle William disagreed.

Though the former's anger rose to considerable eloquence, Uncle William said never a word but lay back in his armchair, smoking his inevitable pipe. At last my father left the room in high dudgeon. Uncle William removed his pipe from his mouth just long enough to say to me in an even tone: "I'm not going to quarrel with old Herbert!"

Uncle Bertie's brand of humour on the other hand was a trial to Aunt Lizzie and to all of us. Even Uncle William, loyal as he was, found his brother a strain, though the blood tie between them spared him the extremes of impatience which Aunt Lizzie strove to suppress during the long visits her brother-in-law paid them in the summer. My charitable mother was the one that bore with him best, but then all she saw of him was an occasional call when he was at home in Edinburgh. She put his foolishness down to his having lived long years with an aged mother and gradually getting into the habit of speaking cheerful nonsense to her. Uncle William put it down to his prolonged celibacy. If a silence should chance to fall, and it was apt to when Uncle Bertie was among us, he would suddenly remark in an enquiring tone: "Goodle-Oodle?" If this proved a sterile opening he would hopefully add: "Honest Fellah!" Nothing however can be gained by reviving Uncle Bertie's foolish repertoire. The above will sufficiently explain how it came to pass that when he brought one of his visits to a close he was scarcely out of the house when Uncle William, a white-haired old gentleman, and Aunt Lizzie, stout and grey-haired, would find themselves waltzing round the dining-room table for very joy.

Uncle Bertie had, however, one great quality. He made the most beautiful model yachts. As no young person was encouraged to come near them they roused no interest in us, though he did, I believe, organize a yearly regatta. Actually there was one exception, and he was a member not of the

Grierson family but the Ogston, our cousin Sandy (Alexander) Ogston. I once stayed with him when he was President of Trinity College, Oxford. Going upstairs one day I noticed a beautiful model yacht exposed on the landing and asked him what it was. He told me that when he was about sixteen he had asked Uncle Bertie to sell him one of his yachts, which Uncle Bertie did, charging only what the materials had cost him. This came to me as something of a shock. I had not known that Sandy knew Uncle Bertie. Who, I now asked myself, who had been the fool: Uncle Bertie or ourselves?

Symbister House is now a school. When my uncle and aunt died within a year of each other their only child, a daughter, was living in Vancouver and had no wish to come back and settle in the old house on Whalsay. It was an oddly civilised house to be standing on beautiful barren Whalsay. The story was that the Bruces originally lived in the big farmhouse at the foot of the hill, but that Uncle William's grandfather, who was on bad terms with his son, built a new house on the hilltop where the winds are wildest, to spite his heir. I had curious confirmation of this story from the man I sat next to at a UNESCO dinner shortly after the war. His name was Nicolson and he was a Shetlander. We spoke of our common acquaintances and I told him the family tradition about the building of Symbister House. He said there was more truth in it than I seemed to realize. He could remember his own grandfather telling his father how he had met "old Bruce" in Lerwick and said to him: "That's a fine house you're building on Whalsay!" To which "old Bruce" replied: "Yes! I reckon they won't find that so easy to get rid of as they would the money it's costing!"

And what a fine house it was with its beautiful plaster and wood work. The best materials had been used for everything, excepting only the pillars of the porch. They had been ordered from Aberdeen of the finest Aberdeenshire granite, but they were lost or broken to pieces on the journey north in one of the terrible storms so common on the Pentland Firth that captains were warned, so my father told me, to trim their ships for storm before even entering the Firth. The pillars were replaced with iron ones and they were the only detail of the house that was not of the first quality. The furniture, too, as I said earlier, was beautiful and in every bedroom was an old four-poster bed with carved columns. Although I myself only visited Shetland once, my sisters often spent their summers there. I shall never now go back. Even if I were much younger and fit to travel, I could not bear to see the beloved house turned into a school. As a house it was relatively short-lived, but I believe it accumulated within its walls more happiness than many houses know in a longer spell of time. There are no Bruces of Symbister left today, but the last of them bequeathed something to everyone who sojourned under their roof: for they gave them a glimpse of a way of life that was not always stretching feverishly forward into the future, but was lived fully in the day-to-day present, and a taste of what hospitality should be. I remember Letty saying to me in 1939, just before the final crisis that led to the last war: "You should take François to Shetland, before it is too late. It's the best thing our family has to offer". I followed her advice and we spent that last August with Uncle William and Aunt Lizzie at Symbister. My husband came to be known on the island as "the man who had never seen a whale". He did, however, see his first and last whale before we left Shetland and set out to face the apocalypse.

CHAPTER SIX

The Goblin Picnics

To return to Grandpapa's family, though we were fond of all
our aunts we made in our minds a clear distinction between
the children of the first and those of the second family. Of the
former three were alive when I woke to consciousness, my
mother, Aunt Flora and Uncle Walter. Uncle Hargrave, the
eldest, was killed in the Boer War. For a long time that was all
we were told, but our mother eventually loosened up and
gave us the salient facts. They cast something of a shadow on
our feeling for Grandpapa, though we laid most of the blame
on our step-grandmother. Uncle Hargrave, it seems, was sent
away to school but was provided with no pocket-money. He
was expelled for having stolen a small sum from a school-
fellow, and when he reached home in disgrace he was turned
away by his father and stepmother. He did what, I suppose,
was the only thing he could do in the circumstances. He went
and "served before the mast", a bitter cure for one of the
classic ailments of a childhood starved of affection. It came as
a terrible shock to my mother: Uncle Hargrave had been her
chief friend and ally. She never saw him again. The story went
on to tell that Grandpapa met his son again by chance during
the Boer War and that a reconciliation took place shortly
before Uncle Hargrave was killed in action.

Aunt Flora was always Grandpapa's favourite child, or so,
with no resentment whatsoever, Uncle Walter claimed. She

justified her father's affection by devoting her life to him when his second wife died. Her own brief marriage had come to an end by then through the death of her husband.

As I said earlier, my mother's stepmother kept her in the nursery till marriage set her free at the age of twenty-eight. Aunt Flora was her chief companion in misfortune but better protected, no doubt, by her stepmother's awareness of her husband's preference. However that may have been, my mother with her gift for catching a glimpse of silver through the blackest cloud (and I would place optimism high on the list of virtues that go to make a good mother), assured me that they had their compensations. Pressed for examples, she would offer their having been free to sit with their feet in the fender of the nursery fire, a thing our father never tolerated in us, and allowed to choose their cakes for nursery tea. She could find nothing else, but I believe they must have had many a laugh, possibly at their stepmother's expense, for Aunt Flora and Uncle Walter had both of them a strong sense of humour provided Grandpapa was not the butt, and Mother dearly loved a giggle even in her old age.

In the endless stories Letty and I used to weave together and whose heroines we were, we never saw ourselves as our parents' children. The mother we chose was Aunt Flora, not in my case because I in any way regretted the parents we had, but because the whole point of a story is to make everything different. Only quite recently I discovered that Letty's point of view was different. There was some sense of an affinity with Aunt Flora which seems to have been stronger than the link that bound her to our mother. What is certain is that we both sensed our aunt's sorrow at never having had a child.

She was a tall woman, Aunt Flora, with auburn hair, who in her youth had been a beauty. Indeed, my father, when he met the "Ogston girls", was torn between her and my mother.

Both were beauties; but my father told me himself that it was Mother's gentleness and her love of poetry that very soon settled his choice. Flora kept her beauty of bone till the end; the lines life drew on her face were of self-mastery and humour. Hers was not an easy life. While still living in Aberdeen she had loved and been loved by a married man, as my mother eventually told me. They strove to overcome their feelings and avoid meeting too often, but suddenly Aunt Flora would be moved by an irresistible force to leave the nursery fire and go out in a given direction. On these occasions she always met the man she loved. They would exchange a few words and that would be all. So my mother led me to understand and I can easily accept it, knowing how things were at the time. The urge that had sent her out was a part of a gift Aunt Flora had which was to us a constant source of awe and interest, the gift of second sight. There were countless stories about her uncanny intuitions and foreshadowing dreams. Whether after the death of the man she eventually married or before her marriage I am not certain, but at some point she did social work for a time with Mrs. Sidney Webb in London. She was seconded by a secretary, a young woman who soon developed a passion for her and was apt to make hysterical scenes. One night Aunt Flora dreamed that she went as usual to Mrs. Webb's office and began to go through her correspondence, putting on one side the letters Mrs. Sidney Webb would have to deal with herself, and on the other side those she herself could answer. As she was thus busied the typist, who worked at a small table in the same room, arrived and began to make one of her emotional scenes, accusing Aunt Flora of coldness and so on. Aunt Flora answered her as best she could, assuring her there was no hostility on her side and that the girl was imagining things. To convince her she laid her hand gently on the girl's shoulder. The typist turned ... and bit it. This very naturally woke Aunt

Flora up. She rose unwillingly from her bed and prepared for her day with the unpleasant feeling that she was sleep-walking. She went to her office and began, just as in her dream, to sort out Mrs. Sidney Webb's letters. Just as in the dream, the typist arrived and began the very scene of the nightmare. The moment came at last when Aunt Flora began her well-intentioned, reassuring speech, and as she drew to a close she felt her hand move towards the girl's shoulder and could do nothing to prevent it. The typist turned and kissed it.

A last example of Aunt Flora's uncanny gift occurred during the 1914–18 War. Grandpapa had volunteered to join the British Ambulance Unit as surgeon and he operated behind the Italian lines for about fifteen months although he was over seventy at the time. Aunt Flora went with him and on one occasion, when they had to shift their quarters during a retreat, their unit was lodged in what looked like two adjoining houses thrown together to form a single building. The morning after their first night in their new quarters Grandpapa asked Aunt Flora casually how she had slept. She admitted that she had slept badly. All night long she had been disturbed by a sort of gibbering sound through the wall of her room, as of people talking all at once in an incoherent manner. Grandpapa made no comment. It was some time later that he told her the house beyond her bedroom wall had been a lunatic asylum, only recently evacuated.

Aunt Flora's husband, Uncle George, is to me only a vague if a delightful memory. He was a second cousin of the Ogstons and had apparently been in love with Aunt Flora some years before they married. They probably met when Aunt Flora went to live in London to escape her impossible love affair. When she at last decided to marry her cousin he was already dying of consumption. His name was George Carter and he was a gifted architect. Eric Gill speaks of him at some length in his autobiography. In this account of him I am merely telling what I gathered from my mother's occasional confidences. The only facts I know are their marriage and his death.

Looking back, what my own memory had captured is the image of a pale, elegant figure lying on a sofa beside the drawing-room window of Langcroft. No; it was the dining-room window, but Aunt Flora had arranged it temporarily as a sitting-room. That was during the only summer when we ourselves were not in occupation of Langcroft but had been bedded out in one of Grandpapa's farms to make room for the Carters. Not long afterwards Uncle George died. I must have been very young at the time and all that was left to remember him by were the hooks on either side of the window that had held the mosquito-netting with which Aunt Flora protected him, as he lay, against the mosquitoes which rose in clouds from the marshland beyond the croquet-green; and a delightful water-colour he did for Molly, which showed himself sitting at a little table with his back half turned, painting that very water-colour while behind him a number of irresistible goblins are making off with his apparently innumerable and variegated ties.

And that brings me to one of the most important occasions of our summers at Dinnet, the Goblin Picnics. I only recently learned from Molly who, as our eldest, knew Uncle George well, that they were his invention. I believed them to be as integral a part of our family tradition as our picnics at Muchalls and Dunnottar. The first goblin picnic I remember was given by Aunt Flora, but it must have been after Uncle George's death for he played no part in it.

There were two lochs in our world, Loch Davan, one half of which belonged to Grandpapa, and Loch Kinnord which I believe belonged to his neighbour whose name escapes me.

Loch Davan was only a field-length away from Langcroft, in a hollow to the left of the road that ran past the grounds of Glendavan, Grandpapa's house. Loch Kinnord, where the picnic took place, was no doubt the lovelier of the two, though both were beautiful. It was grown about with birch trees and on its shadowy waters lay several small islands on one of which stood the ruins of what tradition held to have been the hunting-lodge of King Malcolm Canmore. We loved the loch for its beauty, but for us a breath almost of witchcraft and the evil eye rippled its surface and we knew as soon as we knew anything that these islands were inaccessible, as inaccessible as though they lay in the Aegean, and that we must never so much as dip a dusty toe in the lake's gently lapping waters; for Grandpapa had once and for all pronounced them to be haunted by leeches. We had none of us met a leech outside Wordsworth's Leech Gatherer, but we had lively imaginations and nothing would have induced us to disobey.

When I went to this first goblin picnic I had no expectation of its being in any way unusual, and when after our picnic tea Aunt Flora suggested a walk through the birch wood I was unwilling to follow; I would rather have stayed playing by the loch. But I obeyed, though I was one of the last to reach the clearing where the miracle had been prepared; a tree in the middle of the clearing (or was it the marvel of it that set it apart in my memory from the other trees?) stood hung with presents for every person there. It was to a child a breath-taking sight and I had no difficulty at all in believing what I was told, that it was the work of goblins who had been busy while we were having tea.

There were several of these picnics every summer, offered by whichever uncle or aunt had decided to do the work and foot the bill, and each time the presents would be arranged in a different manner, depending on the degree of imagination the donor of the picnic possessed. I remember those of my godfather, Uncle Walter, as the best of all. The glamour of wealth garnered in the mysterious East (for years his home was in Bombay) hung about him and all his comings and goings. What is more and what is better, he loved children. I believe too that the gloom of 252 Union Street, his father's town house, by compensation loosed the reins of his imagination, as it had done for my mother, and whittled to a delicate edge his sense of what befits a happy childhood. Not even rain daunted him when there was a goblin picnic pending. I remember one that took place round a tea-table. The goblins had been busy with the floral table-decorations, and when the time came my hand was guided to a golden chrysanthemum from whose heart I plucked a fire-opal set in a platinum brooch! I had no idea what platinum was but imagined it must be something even more precious than either gold or silver. On another rainy occasion he grouped chairs and rugs to form a bear's den in a corner of the room. Sandy, his first child and son, referred to in the last chapter, and then about three years old, was hidden within, all except his small hand disguised in a huge fur glove which emerged to hand the presents out.

But Uncle Walter's outdoor picnics were the best. He once went the length of composing with balls of twine a great spider's web in the Home Wood. Each guest was given the end of an Ariadne's thread to follow, with his or her name attached to it so that no mistake was possible. It led the owner first through the web, in and out of the other threads, then beyond it into strange places. The path each had to follow was in perfect keeping with his or her age and ability and not all, though some, led the follower up a tree.

The First World War killed our goblin picnics as it killed much else that was innocent, enjoyable and, seen from our present technological and sophisticated viewpoint, no doubt frivolous. I was nine in the summer of 1914 and we were gathered as usual in Langcroft. I suppose it was on August the fourth that the news we were at war with Germany reached us. Letty had been taken to Aberdeen by our mother because she was suffering from toothache. When they returned, Letty with a still swollen cheek and instructions to poultice the offending gumboil with dried figs soaked in boiling water to bring down the swelling, Mademoiselle Schoepfer was superintending my going to bed by candlelight, in the room under the eaves where the three youngest of us slept. Mother came in with a grave face and told us the news. I remember the feeling of panic that seized me. The vision I had was of street fighting and wholesale slaughter in our quiet city of Aberdeen, with its granite buildings that sparkled in the sun (when sun there was) and its friendly smell of herring.

Mother reassured me, as she always did. There would be no fighting in Britain. It would all take place on the far side of the cold protecting sea: in France and in Belgium. I took for granted that the French and the Belgians were made of sterner stuff than I. Some heroic quality born of their troubled history had prepared them, as I was not prepared, to face what was to come. I was not so far wrong, as I was to discover when, twenty-five years later, war caught me out at last on the wrong side of the Channel. In the meantime, at the sound of my mother's ghost-dispelling voice I had let myself slip back into the waters of security, and for years habit of mind and wishful thinking allowed me the illusion that though our world had suffered a severe shock, given time the ship would right itself; for though the goblin picnics were gone, their place was soon taken, thanks to our Swiss governess, by the search for edible mushrooms. They were to become a source of comparable pleasure because here too was a feeling of the gratuitous and unexpected.

It is easy to pin such memories down, but the real joy of Dinnet life is harder to convey. It was its very texture, its ordinary everyday texture, woven of sounds and smells. On waking to another day of glorious freedom there was the clink and squeak of the garden gate as the milk-boy opened it, clanking his milk cans; the brisk swish of the housemaid's brush as she swept the stair carpet; the fragrance of boiling oatmeal and of toast, and the breath of last night's candles; there was the walking on the loose stone walls of the Three-Cornered Field, Alice, Letty and myself, each telling herself a story, each so familiar with every stone, the firm and the wobbly, that we could pass one another swiftly by when we met, with a rare mastery of equilibrium and only a light hold on each other's elbows – we called it waltzing; there were the bicycle-rides to the neighbouring town of Tarland to have tea in the stuffy hotel (sixpence each for as much as we could eat of scones with butter and jam and of cake), or buying short-bread at the Tarland baker's and, oddly enough, yellow, oval Spanish melons which they also sold; there was the celebrating of Letty's birthday which fell on the seventh of August – a lunch of boiled farm chicken with oatmeal stuffing, bread sauce, and green peas from the garden, followed by strawberries and cream, and for tea raspberry vinegar (I never met it anywhere else) and birthday cake.

Farther afield there was the smell of bog-myrtle down by the lake when we loosed Grandpapa's boat from her moorings in the boat-house in the quiet of evening, and the rattle of the chain as it slipped over the boat's side, startling the starlings that rose in a twittering cloud from the reeds and went streaming down the sky. Even the rainy days, even they were a part of our joy, for we were made free of the dining-room table (normally we were forbidden the house and garden for fear of disturbing our father at work) and set to painting pictures. To crown all, we lived at such close quarters with our parents that I was less teased, though I can remember, when I was very small, being once induced to jump on a dead eel my sisters had found on the lake's shore.

All through my life I have drawn draughts from the well of that summer happiness. Even now I need only close my eyes to find myself once more waking and lying drowsy under the low friendly eaves while the household sleeps. Then the thought of the outside world spurs me awake and I steal out of bed and away with only a waterproof over my bathing-dress. Down on tiptoe to the drawing-room, and out through the window, pausing to bury my nose in the tea-roses that grow against the wall. They are full of dew and the chill night has stolen their scent. Then, as long ago, I slip through the treacherous creaking garden gate and across the road to the Three-Cornered Field. Thereafter blindfold my bare feet would know the way, first along a few yards of rough hard road, then over the iron gate and agonizingly down through the pine-trees on the dead cones and needles of countless years, till they reach the bed of dry rushes that are softly brittle and moist with foam at the lake's edge. They hasten now on this easy ground till they carry me to the point where our burn flows into the lake. There I let fall my waterproof and wade out through the cold, cold water, along the glittering path traced by the rising sun, and my heart spills over with that strange compound of joy and anguish which is the very essence of delight.

CHAPTER SEVEN

God's Time

The first and last of life are lived in elemental time, what Jean Follain the poet called "God's time". Perhaps that is why I find it difficult to fit my memories into any rational chronological pattern. Ticking time is Man's time and it goes faster and faster; but underneath there is this elemental rhythm whose slow-swelling waves, like the waves of the sea, seem to advance, but whose substance is in fact always there. Put it another way: in old age we can look back over our past as if it were an immensely long and intricate tapestry from whose uncertain design a continuity gradually emerges which seemed lacking in the fevered beat of ticking time. The mistakes we made, the mishaps that befell us, by the sudden rude intrusion of a clashing colour mar the design, but little by little after a few false starts they become integrated in the harmony of the whole, as though the rat in the maze had taken a wrong direction and then turned back. Or been turned back?

When I was nine years old a very small minor mishap occurred which was to have lasting effects because it laid its horrid finger on a weak spot in my nature. I was playing one afternoon in the garden with Alice and Letty. We avoided playing in the sand-pit for fear of dirtying our identical tussore silk dresses we had been put into for some occasion which was to occur later in the afternoon. Instead we took turns on the swing, and when that palled Alice, always the moving spirit, soon had Letty vying with her at jumping over its wooden seat. They suggested I should try what I could do. I did, but lacked confidence and fell in such a way as to break a front tooth against the wooden seat, and all but break its neighbour.

I was rushed howling and bleeding to our Swiss governess, our mother being at the time out. The causes of my howling were multiple. I was in a good deal of pain and so terrified of blood that the mere sight of the word in print made me quail, let alone the salt taste of my own blood in my mouth. I was in despair at having broken a permanent tooth; I knew Nature could do nothing more for me. I was also alarmed at the thought of what my mother would say when she came home and found that I had, as I imagined, ruined my new dress.

Mademoiselle laid me on my bed and attempted to bathe my mouth with cold water, but I would scarcely allow her near me. My lip was cut and rapidly swelling and I was afraid to let her look close lest she discover the damage to be more serious than I could bear. And so I lay and howled for my mother to come home. I expected her to lay even this double ghost of a ruined dress and a broken tooth.

She came at last, and reassured me at once as regards the dress; but I could read on her face an anxious fear that I had jettisoned my looks. Dr. Gordon, our family doctor, was sent for, as he was in every crisis. He reassured my mother by saying that in all likelihood I could have the tooth crowned. My howls redoubled. I saw myself saddled for life with a false tooth, no more no less. I thought that now no man would look at me, or if he did then I would have to confess my shame and see him turn sadly away. On this most essential point I could not beg even my mother's reassurance, being too ashamed to admit how preoccupied I was with the thought of my future love-life. I suspected she would feel it a little premature and that she and my father would giggle over me secretly in their room at night. As things were, never having read *My Lady Bellamy* she had no notion what hopes I had formed.

Wretched days followed. My lip was not only badly cut; the nerve in the broken tooth was exposed. Even so, a few days of pain I could have borne, especially as I had temporarily become the centre of interest. It was the long years that followed, with dentist after dentist striving to find a solution to my problem, that put me to the test.

As soon as the worst of the swelling had subsided I was taken to the first of these, Dr. Soper, and the occasion afforded me the only moment of deep satisfaction I have ever known in a dentist's chair. My mother protested that what the broken tooth exposed could not possibly be the nerve; it was far too big. Dr. Soper assured her that indeed it was the nerve, and that children's nerves are bigger than adults', which is why children's troubles should never be taken lightly. A fleeting feeling of triumph was the only good I ever got out of that tooth.

Just as Dr. Gordon had foreseen, the dentist crowned the root. It lasted a year. At the end of that time I knocked my mouth against Letty's head in a wrestling match. I noticed nothing at the time, but the next morning I felt with my tongue an almost imperceptible fissure down the front of the tooth. In the course of the day the crown fell apart. All might yet have been well if the broken tooth had been replaced by one similar; it was not certain I would again knock my mouth against Letty's head. Unfortunately the dentist decided otherwise. He replaced the tooth by one of thin porcelain backed with a solid gold support cemented into the root. The idea was that when the next accident happened all he would have to do would be to replace the porcelain front. The trouble was that it too lasted only a year.

From then on, year in year out, I lived with this problem. I never woke but I ran my anguished tongue across my tooth to discover whether or not the dreaded fissure had appeared while I slept, and as often as not it had, for I had developed a fatal tendency to grind my teeth. We moved to Edinburgh without having solved the problem and our first Edinburgh dentist, a jovial man whose chief interest was cricket, succeeded no better than Dr. Soper. The root of the tooth had received such a shock when I broke it that he was afraid to remove the pivot and gold backing and start the whole thing anew. He was soon reduced to despair by the regularity with which I reappeared in his consulting-room with a gap in front of my mouth where an ugly piece of blackened gold was all that remained of his latest effort. At the sight of me he once sank down onto the floor in what he considered a humorous expression of dismay. It did not make me laugh and it nearly made me cry. By the time – I think I was sixteen – I was taken on the advice of friends to a first-class dentist, who removed the pivot, bound the shattered root with gold and solidly crowned the whole, I was marked. Always self-conscious, I was now so to a morbid extent. Although I was naturally athletic I had given up all games except tennis, fearful of breaking my tooth. And what is more, what perhaps is worse, I could never again be persuaded to smile for a photographer or anyone else, because I had discovered that even my newly crowned tooth photographed badly.

But I have run on ahead. Fortunately not all the winds that swelled my early sails were adverse. When I was seven I ran into one which gave purpose and direction to my dreaming. It was also the occasion of discovering what a miracle friendship can be. It was in the autumn of my seventh year that I persuaded my parents to send me to school, though by their standards it was a little early. I would otherwise have been alone in the schoolroom. Letty had outgrown Smithums' lessons and had joined her elder sisters at the Aberdeen Royal High School for Girls. Poor Smithums had a progressively difficult time with us and had gradually been reduced to bribing Alice and Letty, and perhaps even myself, with prizes to get even a semblance of effort from us. It is never a good thing and with us it was deplorable. Instead of appreciating her generosity as we might well have done, with the clear eyes of youth and its heartless lucidity we recognized the method for what it was and thought the less of her for requiring such bolstering up of her authority. Obviously even for me the time had come for a change. And so to school I went in the mistaken belief that this new door which was opening before me was the gate to liberty. By the time I awoke to the truth it was too late to retract.

My first friend was a year older than myself. She too was called Janet. She lived in a street parallel to ours and linked to it by a lane that ran past our garden gate and past our back door, which was actually on the side of the house. We soon took to walking home from school together, and when we reached Desswood Place, where she lived, I would persuade her to come the whole way by promising to lend her a book. The next stage was that I would suspend fulfilment of my promise till we had done another *aller-et-retour* between our house and Desswood Place, thus prolonging our time together and retarding the moment of homework; for I was never studious. Not in those early days. It was a thing I had forgotten, but Janet reminded me of it when, after having lost sight of each other for a quarter of a century (partly due to the war), we met again for a meal in a Paris restaurant. But what I do clearly remember is how once she stood waiting at the back door while I ran upstairs to beg my mother to invite her to spend a night with us as a real guest, sleeping in the four-poster bed in the spare bedroom in proper style. My mother laughed, but she agreed to the plan and a few days later Janet accompanied me along the lane with no persuasion, and we had the whole evening together. Then I in my turn was invited to spend a night in her parents' spare bedroom.

My friendship with Janet was, as I said, my first experience of friendship; but there was another girl in our class at school whom I longed to know because she fascinated me by some quality difficult to define, that set her apart from the other girls. She was always at the top of the class or near it, though a year younger than myself. She had blue-black hair cut short where the rest of us had mouse-, carrot- or corn-coloured pigtails, and her family name was Ludwig. Even at that early age I had a taste for the exotic, perhaps from living as we did between two languages. But above all she gave me the impression that she possessed some quality I longed to share but was incapable of defining. It had nothing to do with money or social status. What perhaps I sensed was that she came of a background in some way analogous to our own but different, something I was faintly aware of missing in the other girls.

The day came at last when I succeeded in luring Margaret – that was her name, and she was to become the wife of Herbert Read, the art critic – in her turn along the lane and home with me. I took her up to the drawing-room where my mother always sat in the late afternoon, and almost at once our little upright pianoforte drew her. She played us the first page of Beethoven's *Moonlight Sonata* by heart but could go no further. She explained to us that she had picked it up by ear from hearing her mother play it. She sat still for a moment, her long unchildlike fingers resting on the keys, and my mother asked

her what she wanted to be when she grew up. She turned her
round childish face towards us. Under eyebrows as delicately
traced as a Japanese skyline her large blue eyes had suddenly
lighted up. Unhesitatingly she answered: "A composer!"

And so Margaret became for years the most important person in my life, and her family a sort of cultural milieu in
which some of the best things in me blossomed. The Ludwigs
were my world, my discovery, which meant that their
influence was probably even greater than my own family's.
Margaret has often told me that she had been as strongly
marked by the atmosphere my father distilled, an atmosphere
I have never forgotten. But the Ludwigs had an advantage
which was lacking to us in those early years, or at least to the
three youngest of us. They lived in closer daily contact with
their parents than we did through not being screened from
them by nurse and governess, and I think that is important.

Both Margaret's parents were half Scotch and half German.
Her father was in some export-import business – the name
"Hamburg" surges up as through a mist – I never knew what.
It was not important. What counted for him and for all of
them was music. He was a slender man who seemed tall seen
from what was then my level, distinguished by a beard cut
short and shaped to look rather like the old-fashioned side-
whiskers. He had a strong sardonic sense of humour and
although he was on familiar, easy terms with his children he
had a great deal of authority and his word was law. Mrs.
Ludwig was a thin, lively little woman without an atom of
beauty when I knew her, but with a warm cheerful manner
that endeared her to me at once. She came to be one of the
people I best loved as a child and beyond. I never saw her out
of temper; self-pity was an emotion she was too selfless ever to
have known. For that matter, she would have seen no cause
for it; children were no burden to her, and music was for her

rather the stuff of life than a career to be pursued. Nor was the love she had for her two sons and six daughters either exclusive or possessive. When I came to stay with them, as later I often did, I never felt on a different level from them. She simply opened the door a little wider to include me too.

Mrs. Ludwig played the pianoforte and her husband the violin and each of their children was set in turn to learn some instrument, though it was not till much later that they managed to play string quartet among themselves. Margaret, who played both pianoforte and violin and was later to take up the viola and learn to conduct, was musically the pearl of the family; but Violet, the second daughter, was full of promise as a pianist and dreamed of becoming a concert player.

Looking back on the excitement of the long period of initiation which followed my introduction to the Ludwig family, I sometimes wonder whether the advantage children enjoy today of having only to turn a knob or press a button to hear in their own home the greatest music played by the finest performers is not paid for too dearly by two things: the necessary dissociation between music and both instrument and performer where the wireless is concerned, and between player and listener in the case of television, dissociation which incidentally robs them of a fear of disturbing the player that can be instrumental in training a child to listen with both mind and ears; and the too early familiarity with great music which in many cases deprives them of the aesthetic shock of hearing a thing for the first time. Long years ago, Francesco von Mendelssohn, the great-nephew of the composer, chanced to spend a few days with us in Edinburgh when the Klinger Quartet, whose 'cellist he was, was performing there. He told me that the branch of the Mendelssohn family he grew up in was so musical, and so much music was performed in their house, that he seemed never to have heard a thing for the first time. This left him a feeling of frustration and I came to see his point, though at the time I was too inexperienced. For nothing would I have missed hearing Brahms' B flat minor concerto for the first time with D. F. Tovey at the pianoforte, and for the second time with Rudi Serkin, which came as a renewal of that first unforgettable shock. The third time I heard that concerto the pianist was unfortunately Rubinstein, and the shock was the unpleasant one of falling from the level of high tragedy into the morass of romanticism; for where both Tovey and Serkin respectfully harnessed their genius to the composer's intentions as indicated by his often minutely detailed expression-marks, Rubinstein simply let himself be carried away by the gorgeous noise he was making. Or so it seemed to me.

But to return to the Ludwigs, my father had already, through poetry, given us a glimpse of a higher order of reality; in the Ludwig home I discovered that it is possible to lead an ordinary life, full of dull jobs and crawling with children, and yet be illuminated from within. In Mrs. Ludwig's case this inner light radiated into every nook and cranny of a home which but for it would have been no different from a thousand others.

The dreams I now began to dream with Margaret were almost rational dreams, and they were rooted in this new reality of music. Fired by Violet I, too, determined to become a pianist and play in public. I forget at what time I decided it would be in Vienna I would study. I believe it was even before we left Aberdeen for Edinburgh. It was Grandpapa who was unwittingly responsible for my decision. He had studied in Vienna after taking his medical degree in Aberdeen, and the nostalgic look in his eye when he spoke of the Wiener Allgemeine Krankenhaus made a deep impression on me. I associated his nostalgia with the city itself, not with the great hospital, and as soon as I learned that Vienna was as famous for its music as for its medical school I determined I would go there. Oddly enough, when Alice and I did eventually go to Vienna, Alice to study Applied Art and I music, I had once to accompany her to a consultation in Grandpapa's beloved hospital; but the smell of anaesthetic and the sight of wan figures being wheeled across the courtyard so overcame me that I fainted in the doctor's consulting-room. There is always magic in youth, a foolish term no doubt to apply to the razor edge where a child has his being between visual "reality" and an inner personal world whose validity he has as yet no reason to discount; but let it be. For me, much of that magic was rooted in the Ludwigs' house in Rubislaw Den South, one of the then peripheral avenues which, like King's Gate, led gently out of the city to the open country. I used to come whenever possible to stay there after we moved to Edinburgh. I remember one evening in particular when we were both, Margaret and I, on edge with excitement after hearing Violet play the *Waldstein Sonata*. We went upstairs to the bedroom we shared, but not to sleep, though it was late by our homely standards. We were in too great a fever for sleep. Leaving the room in darkness we hung out of the window together, breathing in the fragrance that rose from the shadowy garden below, both of us drunk with visions of our future. It was one of these moments of shared emotion so intense as to be almost unbearable, such as I have never known to that degree or in that context − love is a different matter − with anyone but Margaret. It was probably the most powerful link between us, that we were tuned to the same pitch and responded to the same stimulus.

On another occasion, and in the same mood, I remember wandering with her after dark in search of who knows what adventure. Nothing then seemed impossible. We passed slowly by houses with tree-masked lighted windows and we imagined that beyond them strange dramas were being played out in which we longed to share. From one house in particular there came the sound of gramophone music. We paused by its garden gate and stood wondering what adolescent boys and girls turned and turned to its music; hoping too that some fantastic figure would at length step out from the front-door as from an Aubrey Beardsley drawing (Alice, by then at the Edinburgh College of Art, had just discovered Beardsley), come gliding down the garden path and find us waiting . . . for what? Not, in what was then our mood, for any idle romance, but for some one of the many stars that peopled our imaginary world, to spill over into our here and now.

Some years later, during the Sturm und Drang of youth when I had already been in Vienna for a year and was home again, I was to rush to the other extreme. Then the sight of the long rows of identical houses in certain streets of Britain would drown my spirits in a wave of nausea. There is no other word, though today it has a Sartrean flavour. It seemed to me that I knew what was going on behind each closed window and how the very furniture was arranged. The knowledge sickened me by forcing me to recognize to what poor use we most of us put our lives; nor did I count myself an exception.

Perhaps this nausea lay at the root of the force that drove me forth again. Expatriation is a stimulant. You are no longer hemmed in by convention or custom since the new system of convention and custom you enter you know nothing of, and so escape. What goes on behind French windows is a mystery to me to this day. The feeling of lightness and freedom has remained to me that made it a delight to wander through the Paris streets by night when I still lived there, and now to drive through the Languedoc countryside when evening is falling, and see, on heights beyond the occasional wayside house or group of houses that light you as you go by, on seemingly inaccessible hillsides, here and there a window light up.

But that evening in Aberdeen I still peopled the staid granite houses with phantoms strayed from all I had read of poetry and romance. I still believed that the lightning of adventure could strike and transfigure my life at any moment, in any place.

CHAPTER EIGHT

Dinnet

The need for a complementary self is felt very early in life, independently of any thought of sex. For me Margaret was that complementary self: the mirror that reflects, the tinder that sets alight, the key that opens doors, the well that keeps secrets because it shares them. Nothing new for me was perfect in which she had no part, and I soon persuaded my mother to invite her to spend a summer with us at Dinnet.

I have already given some account of Dinnet, but I have not, as it were, put it on the map.

"Dinnet" for us was the property Grandpapa had bought at some period of his career, and it lay west of Aberdeen, between Aboyne and Ballater. It was not, therefore, an inherited property; for us it yet had a consecrated quality by reason of the three Scotch pine, grown to great size, which Queen Victoria had done my grandfather the honour of "planting" to mark at that point the boundary. This must have happened before any of us children were born.

In point of fact "Dinnet" was above all the name of the station where we left the train which, summer after summer, carried us "up Deeside" to the same cottage (lent us by Grandpapa) in the same garden on the same moors, to the same skyline, the same smells, the same sounds, the same native food and the same country people. We had our roots so deeply embedded in the Aberdeenshire soil – or so we felt – that we seemed a part of all that grew from it and akin to the birds and beasts.

There is a link between the young human animal and the universe, a sort of complicity. We may not be "clear of the nets of right and wrong" (not in the Scotland of my youth) but we are a part of the "mystical brotherhood". I have never recaptured the feeling as the permanent condition it then was, but occasionally its essence emerges from the lines of such a poem as I have quoted, or as Kathleen Raine's "Message from Home". Or it may be that on opening the door of an empty room on a cool spring evening after dark, a room where someone has left the window wide open, the air that meets you is pregnant with so much that as you grope your way into it you seem to take a plunge into some other Time. Every atom of self-sufficiency drops away and you are once more as in childhood a part of a whole; no longer an individual arrogant behind her protecting shell of personality, but a very small, very essential part of a whole of such pleni-tude that even now at the roots of you the lost child skips.

I believe this feeling of being at one with the universe is com-mon to all children; but I believe, too, that the circumstances of our childhood were unusually propitious. Scotland is a country where you can never escape the elements. I sometimes wonder whether it is not for this reason that the Scots are so interested in metaphysics and theology. Or were. Things may have changed. But it seems to me that no one who has lain in bed lis-tening to the winds of Scotland howling in the chimney, or the rains of Scotland beating on the window-panes, or the seas of Scotland thundering against her rocky coast can avoid meditat-ing on first causes and ultimate ends; and although his meditations may lead nowhere conclusive, at least they will have roused in him a sense of glory which might otherwise have remained latent and which can be the key to a great deal.

It was all this that Dinnet represented for us; but it was our mother, with her feeling for ceremony and her knack of turning the simplest event into an "occasion" who made of it, as she did of Christmas, a sort of bedrock which at once bore us up and fed our imagination. It all linked up with her love of what she called "planning ahead". We often mocked this tendency in her, but no doubt careful planning was necessary with five children, a nurse, a governess and three maids to organize harmoniously, and a husband to isolate and protect in his writing hours from any awareness of their presence; a thing she did so successfully that when once an old friend of the family asked W. B. Yeats, during a visit to us in Aberdeen, what he thought of "Grierson's children", Yeats replied: "I don't believe in them!"

Our departure "up Deeside" was the object of such minute planning that today I feel it hard to believe the journey can scarcely have lasted an hour, if that. Seven King's Gate was closed for the summer as carefully as though we were to be a year gone. I can remember waiting in a darkened house that smelled of mothball for the great moment when the horse-cab was to come and carry us children to the station. The hall would be full of wicker hampers, large and small, old-fashioned trunks and even packing-cases. The cat would be spitting and struggling in one small hamper and the sandwiches neatly packed in another. We children would be rushing up and down in our excitement, or gluing our noses to the windowpanes behind the drawn blinds, agog for the first sight of the cab. We kept clear of the grown-ups who, tense with anxiety lest something be left behind, were counting and recounting the trunks and parcels, their nerves already frayed by contact with the travel anguish which made my father burdensome before any journey.

On one dramatic occasion some years before I was born a

very important article had been left behind, the baby. I believe it was Alice, all ready wrapped in her Shetland shawl and placidly waiting on a bed for someone to remember her. She was recovered *in extremis* thanks to our mother's wise habit of reaching the station at least half an hour before the train was due to leave.

We ate our sandwiches and hard-boiled eggs on the train. It was a good idea because it kept us occupied and spared having to feed us either before we left the shrouded house, or after we arrived at the newly-opened cottage. As soon as we had emptied the hamper we would hang out of the windows, breathing in the smell of heather and briar-rose, unmindful of warnings against stray cinders, a frequent occurrence in those days. We knew the names of all the stations by heart and at each a crowd of summer visitors would be waiting on the platform, for there were few trains and their arrival was the event of the day. We felt ourselves in some obscure way different from the ordinary summer visitor. We had a stake in the land and our roots in the soil and we belonged, or so we felt, where the others merely alighted. We also sensed that the grown-ups considered our position as in some way superior. Later on Letty and I came to envy those summer visitors who spent their holidays in an hotel, or "hydropathic" as they were called "up Deeside", presumably for some good reason. We longed to be able to boast at school of having shared in what our riotous imaginations saw as the cosmopolitan life of even Profit's Hotel, near Dinnet station, although we would have preferred a proper "hydropathic", with its white enamel paint, its electric light, and its red staircase and passage carpets.

At Dinnet station we were met by a horse-cart and a pony trap. Our parents and two elder sisters and probably the Swiss governess stepped nimbly up into the pony trap while the rest of us piled into the horse-cart with the luggage for our much slower but equally delightful journey along the dusty white road that ran between two stretches of purple moorland. Only one parallel can give a notion of what we felt – I believe I speak for us all – as we breathed in the familiar smells and rested our town-weary eyes on the familiar landscape. If it were possible for a sponge that had lain a year in the chemist's shop to recover life on being plunged back into the sea, then it would feel as we felt while the slow horse-cart trundled us back into our paradise.

The road ran in a straight line for perhaps a couple of miles (or so it seems on looking back), at which point we turned left into the village of Ordie, past the general store where Mr. Mackle sold everything from calves' foot jellies to tobacco, and a row of cottages, most of them with gay gardens in front. In some of them we had our entry. There was Sandy, the shoemaker, where we had our shoes soled. He lived alone and had so green a thumb that his garden was the loveliest of them all. We were always willing to fetch or carry shoes because he never failed to take us round the flower-beds with him, plucking a flower here and a flower there till he had made us a sweet-smelling nosegay. Then there was a family whose name I forget, with whom we had tea once every summer in their best parlour, and where I remember having had my nose put out of joint by the unexpected presence of that family's latest baby who drew all attention. There was the miller too and his wife, Jean Kynoch. Theirs had been what is called a Scotch marriage. It meant that they had gone before neither minister nor registrar but had simply declared themselves man and wife in front of a witness. In our Swiss governess's eyes they were not married at all and it shocked her that we should be allowed to visit there. But we loved the miller and his wife – speaking for the three youngest of us – and it was to tea with them that we best liked to go. Old Jean made us cream scones which we ate with fresh butter and redcurrant jelly round a plain deal kitchen table set in front of the house. Long, long afterwards – at least forty years – I discovered to my extreme distress that Molly and the Swiss governess had disliked having tea with the miller and his wife because they were dirty! Dirty? So Molly, a mature woman at the time, told me, with sparkling eyes. I was staying with her in Cambridge at the time, with the Second World War behind us. I was appalled; for Alice, Letty and I had still been at the age when people were personalities rather than bodies. Your heart went out to them or it didn't. There was no dissecting.

Lastly there was the blacksmith. He had married a gypsy and had a host of black-eyed children with grubby faces and clothes but with a wild charm about them. My father always said the blacksmith was an intelligent man. He used often to drop in on him and lend him newspapers. I remember the smithy as both beautiful and terrifying. There was the fearfulness and foreignness that iron has for little girls, whether it be cold or red-hot, the frightening stamping of the horses and their beauty, the hideous smell of their smoking hooves when the red-hot nails penetrated them, the glory and majesty of the fire when the bellows blew it into flame. When I lingered there it was with feet ready for flight.

Once the village of Ordie was ·behind us the way ran between low stone walls masked here and there by broom and eglantine. Beyond the wall to the left lay the marshland where we were forbidden to go. At the point where the lane turned at right angles, skirting the base of the Three Cornered Field till it met the Dinnet road again in front of the Home Wood, stood Langcroft, the cottage lent us by Grandpapa.

By the time we reached it the grown-ups had started unpacking in front of the house, and the village carpenter was opening the packing-cases while our father had brought out his fishing-rod and was practising casting, the broad path serving as a river. We children would leave them to their occupations and be off on our round of recognition, like dogs reconnoitring familiar surroundings. First up to the bedroom where the three youngest of us slept, till Alice made herself a diminutive room in the box-room halfway upstairs. There we rummaged in the window-seat-toy-box among the rudimentary toys which were all we kept in Langcroft, and all we needed, with so much else to entertain us; then down to the croquet-green which lay a little below the house, sheltered from the outer world by a screen of trees and fenced off from the marshland where the mosquitoes bred that were our only torment. The carpenter by this time was busy putting up the wooden framework of the open "Japanese" tent where our father worked during the summer. We then hastened back, past the house and out through the garden gate and along the lane to the Home Wood to see whether our kingdom was intact. I remember how once all four of us, Flora, Alice, Letty and myself, climbed each a separate gean tree and were eating as many geans as were compatible with singing, at the top of our voices, the Barcarolle from Offenbach's *Tales of Hoffmann*, when the gong sounded from Langcroft announcing that tea was ready. It was another of those moments when happiness so overfilled me as to be almost unbearable.

When we climbed down in obedience to the gong I remember questioning Flora about her recently diagnosed short-sightedness. I asked her what the world looked like to short-sighted eyes; in other words, at what point it ceased to be visible and what became of it. She explained with her usual lucidity that just as when I looked across the moors to Morvan, our highest hill, I saw all the details blended into a general impression of purples and greens, so she saw what was much closer at hand, but that there was no point at which, as I imagined, things simply ceased to exist.

The most important character in the world that was now ours was, of course, Grandpapa, who ruled us from his house, Glendavan, which stood at the end of a long avenue of Scotch pines. A holy hush hung about the place and lapped you round as soon as you were through the gates. To the uninitiate it was merely the sighing of the wind in the tall pines, the humming of bees on their way to and from the flower garden, the distant murmur of voices from where uncles and aunts were at tea on the verandah, the occasional barking of the shooting spaniels in the kennel behind the house. But we knew better. We knew it was the very breath of the Titan whose avenue this was, whose house this was, whose land this was, and to whom at a last analysis we owed our being.

Grandpapa, your Grandfather, Father: three holy names, the first tentatively affectionate; the second frankly awe-inspiring and usually connected with the conveying of some interdiction as regards our playing stark naked at being Picts in the Pict circles on his moor, or, at a later date, bathing, still naked, in his lake within conceivable sight of what were tactfully referred to as the "farm hands"; the third – and it only concerned the grown-ups – so expressive of the remoteness and respect that tempered the affection borne him by his sons and daughters, our uncles, mother and aunts, that I never connected it with our own father. He had to put up with the homely and undistinguished appellation of "Daddy", though heaven knows we respected him and heaven knows he could be awe-inspiring. But in all things there are degrees.

Yet we loved our Grandfather. I even secretly prided myself on being the one that loved him best, though I had nothing to prove it. Certainly, by the time I was born he had to some extent mellowed. I even occasionally met in him faint traces of humour which gave the more pleasure that they were so unexpected. He was what was called a "man of iron". As a student he had been very brilliant and very wild. So we were told as we grew older and began to ask questions. However that may be, there could hardly have been a greater contrast than between him and my father. Grandpapa was a man of action, whereas my father was a passionate and imaginative scholar for whom poetry was the most important thing in life. But each of them had a very real respect for the other, while considering the other in many of his aspects as something of a joke. Grandpapa's situation was of course the stronger, at least while we were enjoying the use of his cottage and the amenities of his lake and land; but our father kept his end up by a practice of extreme independence. He would work away at his latest book in the tent on the croquet-green, rarely accompanying my mother on her almost daily visits to the "big house". He did occasionally unbend so far as to join a shooting party, thereby providing an element of danger and excitement which would otherwise have been lacking. He would get so worked up when a rabbit shot out of its hole with a ferret at its heels, or a grouse or pheasant rose unexpectedly from the heather at his feet, that he forgot the other guns. On one occasion he followed the flight of a bird with his pointed gun and only fired when he had Grandpapa almost in his line of vision. Grandpapa's chin received a little of the shot, but not so much as deigning to turn his head to see who was responsible (he probably guessed), keeping a stony profile turned on his son-in-law, he wiped the blood from his chin and went on tranquilly waiting for another bird to appear. My father dared offer no word of apology, so clear it was that to take no notice was the only attitude his father-in-law was going to tolerate.

Professor H.J.C. Grierson did, however, get his own back

when Sir Alexander Ogston K.C.V.O. wrote his memoirs of the three campaigns in which he had taken part. The latter submitted his manuscript to his son-in-law's superior literary knowledge, in case it should need a "touch up here and there". As things turned out, my father claimed that he had practically to re-write the whole thing. It so happens that I never read the book, *Reminiscences of Three Campaigns*, until long after I was grown-up and married and a mother of four children. It came as a great surprise to me. I discovered that our "Man of Iron" never travelled without a pocket edition both of the New Testament and of Shakespeare; and that, when held up for lack of transport in a Greek harbour during one of his campaigns, and prevented from sleeping by the fleas, he spent the night reading Shakespeare. Nor would I have thought it possible to evoke landscapes so powerfully without any study for effect but with only the most economical exactitude. Even if my father had some part in rhythm or concision, these were landscapes he had never seen. By the time I read *Reminiscences of Three Campaigns* I had learned some of the facts of Grandpapa's career. As a young man, after taking his medical degree he had specialized in military surgery and had gone, on his own initiative and at his own expense, to Germany, France and Russia to study military conditions there, and compare with our own. On his return, he had risked his career and caused a scandal by denouncing the inefficiency of our military sanitary services. He did so, if I remember rightly, at a dinner of the Royal College of Surgeons. He had been one of the first to practise Lister's methods of antisepsis, in face of great hostility. Again at his own expense and on his own initiative he had taken part in the Egyptian War (1884–1885) and the Boer War in order to gain practical experience of field surgery.

I knew nothing of all this when I was young. I could see he

was a great man by looking at him and I was content to learn about the early period of his life from what little my mother told me. Indeed, for a long time my best hope of an afterlife derived from what she once confided in me – and it was a confidence that came to her directly from her father. It was something that had happened to him when he was lying ill of typhoid fever in a military hospital during one of his campaigns. He had told her that when at his lowest ebb he had several times the clear impression of leaving his body. It would cost him a painful effort to reintegrate that body when the nurses came to tend him. One night he found himself being borne through the air beyond the hospital walls by a rushing wind, and passing others who were being swept along in the same direction, all carrying lanterns in their hands. He even claimed that on one occasion he was present (in the spirit, presumably) during the discussion the doctors were having about his own case, and when one of them declared he would not survive the night he said to himself: "They don't know me!" He was right. He lived to be well over eighty.

On another occasion he admitted to my mother that though he had often been in the thick of battle, he had never felt the taste of fear. Our gentle mother, trying to grasp what it could mean to feel no fear, asked him whether he had been aware or not that he was in danger. He replied rather impatiently that of course he had been aware, and had taken all reasonable precautions, but that he had never known fear until the day he was presented to Queen Victoria.

What Grandpapa felt then was probably akin to what many people felt when first introduced to him. He was so self-possessed and so self-sufficient that he could isolate himself from his surroundings and pursue his thoughts as tranquilly as though he were alone. His silences used to drive me to nervous speech. I would launch forth on some interminable story till for very lack of breath it petered out, when as likely as not Grandpapa, after a moment, would say in kindly tones: "Say it again, my dear!"

Two stories will complete my picture of Grandpapa. The first occurred when he and his sons and daughters, grown men and women at the time, were all to go off on their bicycles for a picnic. While preparations were going forward a discussion arose as to whether Uncle Walter should bring his camera. Cameras in those days were voluminous and required a tripod for their support. Uncle Walter brought the discussion to a close by saying he had no intention of lugging such a cumbersome object on a picnic. Just then the voice of "Father" rose from the hall below: "Walter! You're bringing your camera?" "Good idea, Father!" cried the dutiful son with a sigh, but also with a laugh; for none of Grandpapa's children were really dupes. They knew they obeyed their father's commands because they had no choice but to obey, and their laughter was as much against themselves as against him. All, that is to say, except perhaps my mother, till her husband, and later her children, had plucked the scales from her eyes; and Aunt Flora, who wore blinkers to the end and whom the second story concerns. It was told me by my mother, who by then had come to see the joke.

She had gone up to Glendavan for tea, as she often did, and she was sitting at the tea-table on the verandah with only Grandpapa and Aunt Flora present. Aunt Flora had told her in whispered conference that Grandpapa was suffering from indigestion. He would not have liked it said because indigestion is an unmanly ailment, so Mother was in something of a quandary when her father began to work his way through a plate of macaroons. When only a few remained she murmured under her breath to Aunt Flora that it was perhaps unwise, under the circumstances, to give Father macaroons.

Grandpapa heard what she said, and his profile stiffened, as it did when something displeased him. But he went on peacefully eating his macaroons. Aunt Flora's face stiffened too. In tones of rebuke she answered: "Macaroons don't hurt Father!"

"Good idea, Father!" and "Macaroons don't hurt Father" became a part of our generation's family repertoire of quotations, and were made apt use of on many an occasion.

CHAPTER NINE

Farewell Aberdeen

In 1915 my father was appointed to the chair of Rhetoric and
English Literature at the University of Edinburgh. While his
nomination was pending we were told nothing of our even-
tual prospects, but we sensed some unusual thing in the air
and were agog for information.

It was during this period that the word "testimonial" first
entered our life and it served as a clue. By the time we left for
our summer holidays we had followed it to its source and discovered what was afoot. We also discovered that our father's
age was forty-nine. Hitherto the ages of both our parents had
been kept a secret from us, as was then the convention.

The summer of 1916 was the first we spent away from
Dinnet. I have forgotten why a change was made. It is prob-
able that under Uncle Todd's influence we had begun to
complain and beg to be taken to some new place, though
instinct and native good sense would tell us it would be wiser
not to mention Knokke; there were limits to what we could
expect. Or perhaps, with the vista of a new life opening
before us, we wanted everything to be new. A child is torn
between his imagination which reaches out to the unknown,
and his heart which clings to the familiar.

It was to Blair Atholl we went. The prospect of renting a
house was exciting, especially as the one our parents chose was
advertised as having electricity on its ground floor. For reading

in bed candles were still to be our lot, as they were in Dinnet. We had also, at least Letty and I had, high hopes of romance from our new environment, especially when we got there and found the place full of young men in uniform. Those hopes were to be disappointed, which is perhaps not surprising. We were thirteen-and-a-half and eleven respectively.

Uncle Jimmie's death occurred in the course of that summer, and was a bitter blow to us. An element of salutary recklessness and the latent expectation of some glorious miracle vanished when he died. Their ghost was to haunt several of us ever after, and war with the more reliable qualities that came to us from our mother's side of the family.

Altogether that summer remains to me as a sort of disenchantment. I discovered in my new surroundings how much I had left behind in Dinnet, and I sensed that by our disloyalty we had broken some fragile thing that would never be made quite whole again. A growing suspicion, too, suggested that the sort of excitement I craved is not easily to be found in any Scotch summer resort. Gradually I began to take for granted, what in my time so many Scots did take for granted, that my life would be spent elsewhere. I came to live in a state of mental presbyopia, blind to what lay under my nose, but alert to all that came to me from outside; and a great deal came. In fact, I believe it would be true to say that at about the time when for Earl Grey (wasn't it?) the lamps of Europe were one by one going out, for me their rays had begun, one by one, to penetrate the walls of our schoolroom, first in Aberdeen, then in Edinburgh. I already mentioned English poetry. With it came the English language (with, undoubtedly, an Aberdeen accent; but English for all that); next came German and soon afterwards French and Italian music, while from the start we were free of the treasury of French folk songs. I took it all for granted at the time, but later a chilling thought would force its way. Was Earl Grey right? Did the rays that reached us come from fires effectively quenched, much as the sun's rays would light us long after their source was extinct? It no longer comes. I believe the fires are still there, but where at a given point the light that shone brightest may abruptly sink, at the next it will flare up elsewhere. It may be as far afield as Australia or Latin America or the United States. It is the same light, and it has its source in Europe's dormant volcano.

I came to this conclusion by a rather devious route. I have lived long enough to see Europe's position in the world shift, not once but several times, much as the geological world shifted and new mountains surged up from plain and sea, dwarfing or annihilating the older hills. Europe today is dwarfed, but this intangible thing remains, this climate we call European. I have often tried to clear it of the dross I cling to from mere sentimental habit, and discover why it seems to me so important to be salvaged from the wreck. At first all I found was a feeling for time as something more than mere duration; and a deep respect for what Romain Gary called the "margin", the margin of waste by mechanical standards, the margin of the gratuitous in which all beautiful things are made. I met it in the 'twenties in its simplest form in the cafés of Vienna, where you were suffered to sit and read or write or merely moon, over a single cup of coffee without anyone making you feel you should leave your table free for a more consuming customer. There is something there it would be a pity to lose, a respect for the natural need to assimilate and not merely absorb, a keeping of the balance between artistic creativity and technological efficiency. We shall need it if we are to justify the virtuous noise we are all making in favour of the Rights of Man.

The Rights of Man. That, in fact, was the clue which, when I began to follow it in the early 'sixties, led me to my present conviction. They are claimed to have been in some sort secreted by democracy, the rational mind, and the French Revolution, but it seemed to me as clear as clear that their roots are far older and that it is to Christianity our European culture owes its perennial quality. To Christianity and all that prepared its way, from the Old Testament to the Glory that was Grace. Owes or owed?

I had better return to Aberdeen.

Our time was drawing to a close. My mind is a blank as regards the period between our summer at Blair Atholl and our arrival in Edinburgh. I believe our father went on in advance. The rest of us followed and were scattered among various friends of the family. Letty and I came to perch in a strange household, that of Sir William Ramsay, archaeologist, the old friend of my father's who asked Yeats what he thought of Grierson's children and was told Yeats did not believe in them. What made the household seem strange to us was that Lady Ramsay was a fervent feminist. Her feminism went so far that she would drown the males and cherish the females when her cat had kittens, and she was always ready to take up arms on what seemed to us no provocation at all; for we had none of us ever been made to feel inferior simply because we were girls, even if we had caused a good deal of disappointment when we were born. Our father loved the company of intelligent women and had a great respect for their intellectual capacities. He had us educated as though we were boys. The only difference was that he was more willing, perhaps, than if we had been boys to allow us to follow our inclinations and choose such unlikely careers as painting (Alice) and music (myself); for at the back of his mind there lurked the thought that if we married we would not (not when I was young) have to earn our livings. In his gloomier moments it took the turn I mentioned earlier: if we married it would all be wasted.

Lady Ramsay was not one of the intelligent women whose company he enjoyed, though Sir William was his dear friend. No intelligent woman would have kept so needlessly austere a house, nor fallen back on Letty and me as an audience for her husband when one evening he settled down in the drawing-room to read aloud one of the Gifford Lectures he was to deliver some time later in the season. I recall nothing of the occasion but the rather too upright chair I was put to sit on.

And so we left Aberdeen and the friendly security of its university life. Dinnet, even, retreated into the background to some extent. We did return there once or twice, but there was always one or other of the sisters missing. What did it all amount to? In my case scarcely twelve years out of the eighty-five I have recently reached. Yet I carry it still within me, the very foundation of memory, the arbiter of many of my standards, as regards human relations for example, and the wealth and warmth they can add to ordinary everyday life. But when I look back over a total of nearly sixty years spent in a foreign country, which include a second World War and the experience of enemy occupation, it is especially the poetry of those early years that remains to me, and which I identify with Aberdeen; the gaslight and firelight and the sound of horses' hooves muffled in the snow; the long black slides the children made on the frosty winter pavements where we would pause on our way home from school and, throwing down our school-bags, take our turn at sliding before hastening home for tea; the delight of waking to find the nursery window-panes frozen into abstract works of art in every shade of white; the sound of the rushing wind in the great wych-elms just beyond our night-nursery windows; and through it all, the passionate sound of our father's voice reading us how Othello died and Cleopatra mourned her Antony, or changing his tune and setting our nerves a-dancing to: "Do you remember an inn, Miranda, Do you remember an inn?" till the rhythm broke on "Never more, Miranda, never more", and our spirits sank with his voice to a slow heartbeat, heavy with the sense of doom.

PART TWO

The Lamps of Europe

CHAPTER TEN

Twelve Regent Terrace

When we reached Edinburgh I had still a couple of years to swim in the safe aquarium of childhood. What I first glimpsed through its transparent walls was stimulating, if only because everything was new; but as the feeling of novelty wore off there came a sense of malaise. Things were somehow falling apart. For one thing, though I was not immediately aware of this, the atmosphere in which we lived in Aberdeen had been Edwardian and upper-class. There was, or seemed to be, a pattern into which everyone fitted, and if it did not necessarily make for happiness it did make for a sense of security. In Edinburgh we were suddenly plunged into contemporary middle-class life. What is more, in Aberdeen our social position was so safe we could, I do believe, have lived in any part of the city without incurring contempt; for not only had our mother solid roots in Aberdeenshire, but the Scotch respect for learning was still alive in the granite city. In Edinburgh both money and the Law Courts took precedence over the University's purely intellectual values, and to be respected it was advisable to live, not in the East, but in the West End. My poor mother soon discovered that the house she and her husband had chosen, and could afford, was in the wrong part of the town, a situation which was bound to cloud the horizon of a mother with five daughters to dispose of, even a mother as unworldly as ours.

Yet it was a fine house, not large as houses go, but built in the Adams' spacious tradition with beautifully proportioned rooms and well seasoned woodwork. What was more, it was fitted throughout with electricity and we spent our first days there rushing up and down stairs, switching the lights on and off. It was also beautifully situated, raising its once proud head high above Holyrood Palace, above the Canongate and the Royal Mile, both of them at the time I am speaking of part of the slum quarter of Edinburgh, but today restored and reinstated. Unfortunately it also dominated the north-south railway line, and though the latter ran too far below to be a nuisance as regards noise, the winds blew soot-laden in at our windows and all our dust was coal-black. This farther complicated our mother's life at a time when the munition factories were luring women away from domestic service, never to return.

The fact that we were now as a family of little consequence troubled us children not at all. What did trouble us was that in Edinburgh we received for the first time the full impact of the war as it affected civilians. Our two war years in Aberdeen had done little more than alter the nature of our social lives and introduce some fantasy into school routine, with the Royal High School buildings requisitioned as a military hospital and the school itself split up among various empty private houses. As regards our social life, we were taken to fewer children's parties. Instead we were given pennies to spend at sales of work for this or that war purpose; we attended knitting parties where we were set to knit misshapen scarves for soldiers or sailors; we were taken to "talk French" with wounded Belgians; and on one solitary occasion our father allowed us to sell flags or poppies or whatever it was in the street, a thing we had longed to do but to which, for some reason, he had objected. Best of all, when Uncle Jimmie's ship put in at

Aberdeen harbour (he had joined the Naval Reserve at the outbreak of war) he and a number of his fellow-officers, splendid in their uniforms, would take us to the theatre and even, on one occasion, to dine at the best Aberdeen hotel, a sensational event for the three youngest of us. I remember how indignant poor Molly was to see with what zest we tackled each dish that was set before us, whereas she had been taught – perhaps by Auntie – that good manners required one to skip a course. To make matters worse, the captain, who presided over the table, was delighted with our appetites.

On the negative side, for so long as we continued in Aberdeen, the war only caused us children a few minor inconveniences, though it did add to my night fears the dread of being shelled through the night nursery window by German warships in the North Sea. A blight, certainly, was cast on our Christmas celebrations – it must have been in 1915 – when our mother suggested that instead of having a Christmas-tree we subscribe what it would have cost to some one of the many causes that were crying out for money, and content ourselves with receiving our presents off a table. The blow was a harder one than had been the loss of our belief in Father Christmas. Christmas-trees returned the following year on a smaller scale, but nothing was ever quite the same again, because now we knew that all things are mortal.

The only other blight I remember, and it rankled for longer than I care to admit, was when my mother responded to some Archbishop's urging of the women of Britain to offer up their gold ornaments to be melted down into battleships or some such useful article, by sacrificing a bracelet I coveted and had been promised for when I grew up. I had taken that promise very seriously indeed. It was a broad, smooth bracelet of plain gold that clasped close-fitting round the wrist. Mother thought it old-fashioned. I thought it beautiful, and all the changing fashions I have lived through would have agreed with me.

In Edinburgh, almost from the start the shadow of war blotted out all joy and insouciance from life. What was worse, it destroyed for years our mother's serenity and left her weary and harassed. Prices rose, our Aberdeen house remained for a time unsold although the Edinburgh one was already bought; the spectre of money worries began to stalk our home in the shape of mediocre food, no new clothes and insufficient heating. I have only to open the Pandora's box of memory for there to fly out, before I slam it shut, a vision of Alice, Letty and myself huddled over the dining-room fire one gloomy November evening. Although we shivered, we had repeatedly to shove our chairs back into the outer chill, because of the unexpected way the war coal would explode, sending hot cinders flying. Our mother was with us, patiently busy with her unending darning of socks and stockings. Back from the University, our father glanced in on his way to the study, just long enough to announce the latest disaster at sea or on the front, then, relieved at having shifted his gloom onto our innocent shoulders, he left the room, but not before making an absent-minded contribution to war economy by switching the light off as he went, leaving us in double darkness. The three of us burst into a roar of fury which ended in helpless laughter.

Molly and Flora were by this time what was termed "grown-up". It meant that they wore their skirts ankle-length and their long hair pinned up, and that they suffered more than we did from our lack of becoming clothes. But it meant, too, that they had done with school, and the new world they were entering into shone for us three younger sisters like a distant glimpse of paradise, making us impatient of our prison walls. It came strangely to me when later I learned how differently things had appeared to them. The truth is that it fell to them to have to train their parents in the way all parents must be trained, to adapt them to the changes inherent in the times their children are born into, and recognize as theirs. When Molly and Flora came home from a party they would find their furious father waiting up for them in his dressing-gown, his unleashed imagination prepared for everything save only their safe return. They trained him so well that when my turn came at last he would scarcely raise his head from his book to ask where I was going, looking so festive.

Another handicap Molly and Flora had to contend with was our mother's unworldly innocence. Party dresses she could only conceive of as being of white embroidered muslin ("broderie anglaise"), and except for a single pair of white "milanese" silk stockings, which she had probably not worn since her wedding-day, stockings to her were by their very essence black. It took all Molly's looks to blossom under such circumstances, but blossom, for a time, she did. As for Flora, she soon left for Oxford where she shed her stays and her spectacles and gave free rein to a natural taste in clothes, undaunted by poverty.

But Molly had to stay in Edinburgh. It was impossible to send them both to Oxford, and Flora was so brilliant she seemed the obvious one to go. Molly, with her literary and poetic gifts, had to study English Literature at Edinburgh University under her father. It was not an ideal situation.

But these were minor troubles. The tragic impact of war on Molly and Flora's generation was a different matter. The young men who would have been the right age for them to marry were being killed off with sinister regularity. Molly's admirers came and went, but few came back. Uncle Jimmie's eldest son, Jack, took advantage of his exceptional height and build to deceive the Recruiting Office into believing him eighteen when he was only sixteen. He joined the Gordon Highlanders and was killed two years later in a bayonet charge. In the family Bible, where my father kept it, I found the long, long list of the "Killed in Action" in which Jack's name appeared in the *Scotsman*. These lists were daily; several of my father's most brilliant Honours students were swept away before even we left Aberdeen. Flora, who was just old enough to have a vivid memory of life before the war and beyond the nursery, often told me that our father was never again so gay as she had known him in those early days.

These, with the death that followed of the young man to whom Molly had become secretly engaged, were the hardest blows, and it is not surprising that I have such bleak memories of the first year in Edinburgh.

What we did however gain by the change to Edinburgh, and came to appreciate more and more, was the freedom of the fourteen-acre gardens, beautifully laid out, which were common to the occupants of the three terraces in one of which we now lived. They were reached through a little private garden at the back of each house. With their splendid trees, both for beauty and for climbing – when the head-gardener's back was turned – with tennis-court and miniature golf-course, both of them banned on the Sabbath, this was our world. As these gardens were isolated by high walls from the immoral goings-on, on the Calton Hill beyond, of sailors up from Leith Harbour with their girls, our parents could sit back with a sigh of relief and practise with regard to us the "little wholesome neglect" which our father claimed to be an essential part of a good upbringing.

There Alice, Letty and I would foregather with our friends, but especially with the young men Alice lost no time in drawing round her. Altogether, though scarcely out of our childhood, we evolved for ourselves a glorious, wildly free adolescence whose playground was these gardens, and which owed its very freedom to our being so securely rooted in our parents' love that like acrobats we could, and did, take risks, knowing the infallible net was stretched beneath us. Even so, I doubt whether at the time we realized that we were taking risks.

Perhaps our parents knew more about our goings-on than they let us guess. On how many summer evenings, when the light lingered on so long that we could play tennis till after ten at night, I would escape through my bedroom window when supposed to be in bed, slip down onto the roof of our father's library, and thence to the gardens to join and have some part in Alice's magic circle. The glass-roofed study must at some time have been built onto the house and it stood conveniently just under my bedroom window. Can my father really have failed to hear the sound of my feet, though rubber-soled, when they dropped down onto the leads and followed them round till they reached the low wall from which one could jump down into the garden? Did no one hear the rusty hinges of our garden door creak as I slipped out towards freedom? I never knew; but I am certain my mother suspected nothing. She would never have kept silent. My father may well have laughed to himself, who long ago as a child in Shetland, when his elder brother, our Uncle Jimmie, was expected home from Aberdeen where he was studying Law, would escape from his own father's house in Lerwick to row about the harbour in the white summer night, till the *St. Sunniva* or the *St. Ninian* came to anchor.

CHAPTER ELEVEN

Samalaman

Although "the gardens" were our chief centre of attraction, two new strands were soon to appear in the fabric of our lives to widen our horizon. The first of these found a permanent place in my own private tapestry. The second, which concerned us all, was very different. It would erupt sporadically in a splash of colour and then vanish, only to reappear at a point where the whole design had altered. I shall start with the second strand as the soonest told and the liveliest.

This strand was a man, or rather a boy, when he first rang our doorbell, and his name was Arthur Ryan. Aptly enough, he was a legacy from Uncle Jimmie who had known his mother, and it was with an introduction from her that he arrived one day at teatime. It was probably in 1917, but I find it difficult to give shape to those war years. I remember them as a bleak interlude, immeasurable in time, having a beginning and an end, both as clear in my memory as if by spotlight, but for the rest a sort of magma. What is certain is that Arthur was then a midshipman on board the *Warspite*, and he was to irrupt into our lives every time the *Warspite* came to anchor in the Firth of Forth.

I believe he was sixteen when we first met him, and he looked the veriest schoolboy, disguised in naval uniform, with his questing nose and his joyful face. He had come, that first time, with a couple of fellow midshipmen, and they had been barely half an hour in the house when Arthur decided to make an arc-lamp in our dining-room, with the result that after one blinding flash all the lights in the house went out. He was one of those people who are in some way too big to fit into normal life, but who come into their own in wartime. He was, in fact, a bud from the tree whose finest flower was Churchill.

Arthur loved to entertain my mother with stories about the naval battles he had been in. On that first day he told her, in one and the same breath of delighted enthusiasm, how in one battle all the ship's crockery had been smashed to smithereens and in another (I think it was the Battle of Jutland) a shell had exploded in the ship's arsenal and blown its heavy armoured door open. "Do you know what they found behind it?" he cried, his eyes shining. Mother, expecting to hear of some miraculous escape, shook her head. "A man!" shouted Arthur, "Flat as a pancake!"

Another time, in the enthusiasm of one of his stories – I remember we were all sitting in true Scotch style having afternoon tea round the dining-room table – he paused to ask: "Mrs. Grierson, have you ever dived under a punt?" He got no farther in his story. It was drowned in a wave of laughter. Our mother was the gentlest creature, patient and intelligent, combining the feeling for poetry our father had fostered in her with a scientific bent that had never found an outlet. She had never practised any sport, though I can remember, when I was very small, her asking me on several occasions to sit on her ankles while, clad in a long white lawn nightdress, she lay on the floor and painfully strove to sit up straight six successive times without using her hands. I never ascertained her purpose. She was not even fond of walking, and her husband had the greatest difficulty in teaching her to ride a bicycle. When she was presumed to be proficient he persuaded her to join one of the Ogston picnics which were such a feature of the

The five Grierson girls. From left to right: Letty, Flora, Molly and Alice. Janet, the youngest, stands in the foreground.

CENTRE: Janet as Alice in Wonderland.
TOP LEFT: Father. BOTTOM RIGHT: Mother.

7 King's Gate, Aberdeen.

Regent Terrace, Edinburgh.

Grandpapa Ogston.

'Auntie'.

Cousin Nel.

Uncle Jimmie.

Langcroft, the holiday cottage.

The summer house, Glendavan.

Uncle Walter.

Molly.

ABOVE: Margaret Ludwig.
RIGHT: Donald Francis
Tovey. By permission of the
Reid Music Library,
University of Edinburgh.

summer. She fell off into the ditch at the foot of the first descent, and his immediate reaction was to stand over her, moaning that "every time I begin to enjoy myself Fate deals me a back-handed blow!"

No. Mrs. Grierson had never dived under a punt. She had never even appeared in a bathing-dress.

Altogether Arthur played something of the part of a brother to us, the brother we had lacked. Years later, on one of his lightning visits shortly before the Second World War, as he drove my husband and me at breathless speed round the Devil's Elbow, he was to say to me: "When we first met we were all too young, and when we met again you were all married".

One of the young men Arthur brought to the house was a little older than the others, and far from feeling himself too young, he was soon singing us the Indian Love Lyrics with an amorous eye on Molly. He was the only one of them all whose parents we met. As he was their only child, every time the *Warspite* came to anchor in the Forth they would come north. They were a kindly couple whom we would have liked well enough if the father, a retired colonel of the Indian Army, had not taken such pleasure in reciting us patriotic verse. When they turned up on a visit we would strive to keep the conversation flowing, knowing that at the first pause for breath we would hear the ominous words, uttered hopefully and with only seeming diffidence: "Shall I recite?" Then, scarcely waiting for our quavering encouragement, he would take his place on the hearthrug with his back to the fire – our only source of warmth – and launch forth.

It was all the more unfortunate that I soon discovered I could imitate him to perfection: that indeed I was an exceptionally gifted mimic. It did a great deal to heighten my popularity with the family, and would reduce our mother to guilty giggles she strove in vain to smother. She was more aware than we were of the cruelty that can be the shadow side of laughter. Not that our colonel had any notion of what was going on behind his back. It was the principle of the thing that restrained our mother's laughter, or strove to. And certainly none of us would have liked to hurt his feelings, for the man was kindliness itself. He used, whenever he came to Edinburgh, to take us out to tea or to the cinema. When it was to the cinema he would always pay a preliminary visit himself to whatever film he had in mind lest it should contain what he referred to as "intrigue".

We lost sight of Arthur's friends after the war, when the Navy offered a bonus to those that returned to civilian life. Even Arthur disappeared for many years and all we knew of him was an occasional picture postcard from the Red Sea or the Dead Sea, from India or from West Africa. He seemed to be everywhere. He reappeared as suddenly as ever in 1939 when the smell of approaching war grew irresistible.

The other strand was a family.

Among the people my parents had met since they came to Edinburgh were a lawyer and his wife, Mr. and Mrs. Mackintosh. The link between them and my parents was that their three daughters were, like ourselves, newcomers at St. George's School for Girls, the school chosen for our further education. In spite of its qualification, St. George's was a private school, and no doubt our parents had felt, as many parents have felt before them, that the expense would be justified by our making "nice friends". If so, in our case they were to be disappointed. At the end of the first academic year, Alice persuaded our father that she was no budding intellectual and that her proper place was at the Royal College of Art. As for Letty and me, though at one point we shared an agonizing "crush" for the Head Girl, having learned that a crush was the proper thing to acquire, we made no lasting friends. No one of my classmates seemed to me to have the vital qualities of Margaret, nor Janet's unaggressive integrity, though that is not how I would have put it at the time. A real affection rooted in common memories rather than affinity of mind was, however, to develop between May, the eldest of the Mackintosh girls, and myself. It owed nothing to our school where we were not even in the same class, and but for our parents might never have met.

The Mackintosh girls had received the sort of upbringing we ourselves would probably have been given had we stayed on in Aberdeen, though in our case it would have been tempered by our experience of High School, and by the Grierson leaven stirring in our blood. I said earlier that the air we breathed in Aberdeen was Edwardian, though George the Fifth was already on the throne. The atmosphere of the Mackintoshes' house, which stood not in Edinburgh but in timeless dignity in a large garden in Haddington, continued Edwardian long after the trappings of domestic service that sustained it had fallen apart. In that house they had acquired none of the antennae that help the inexperienced to find their way in the mixed context of even a private school. This was made evident on our very first day when we all filed into the dining-hall for school luncheon. The hall was filled with long tables set at right angles, on the one side to the windows, on the other to a small platform bearing a single smaller table. We had been told we were free to sit where we pleased, and this table looked temptingly aloof; but though we were lunching in a school for the first time, some instinct told my sisters and me to keep clear of it. Not so the three Mackintosh girls. With a whoop of innocent joy they made for it, only to be turned coldly away by the Head Girl. It was, of course, the staff table. It was the sort of trap life never wearied of setting them.

It was on the Sports Day of our first summer at St. George's School that I first met the Mackintosh parents. I was very excited about this event. It was for me a new experience to be at a school where there were playing-fields and organized games, and I had discovered I was fairly good at athletics. A whole new field now opened up to me and I spent my spare time developing my muscles (till my father warned me it would all end by turning into fat), learning to turn somersaults and cartwheels and bend over backwards, and training for the various team games we played on two afternoons a week. Music at this point tended to take a back place.

Mr. Mackintosh was a typical Scot, with all the Scotch love of chill open air and the Scotch itch for land-owning. Some years before we came to live in Edinburgh he and his brother had bought one of the loveliest properties I ever saw. It lay west of Arisaig in the heart of the countryside where Bonny Prince Charlie, the idol of every romantic Scotch child, landed in 1745. Here it was that this Edinburgh lawyer lived his real life for a couple of months a year, fishing and shooting and tramping the moors, as essential a part of the community as the crofters and fishermen who lived there from one year's end to the other, and filling to perfection the place of Laird that existed independently of him, has always existed and will probably always exist in some form or another by some natural law of Scotch country life, but will remain as empty as an empty throne if the wrong man inherits or buys the land.

Mrs. Mackintosh was of English county stock, well-bred and intelligent, but highly-strung and inclined to be irritable with the slow-minded or clumsy. She had strict standards of behaviour but a saving sense of humour through which she could usually be got round; and undeniable charm. On the whole, she was more of an animal- than a child-lover, and on dogs and horses she could expend a wealth of patience which was apt to flag when it came to children. Like most English people, she suffered in her health from the climate of Scotland. No one can love the Scotch climate, but those who are born into it find in it a stimulus which is lacking to them elsewhere. This neither endears it to them nor encourages those that have escaped to return; but if they do return, even temporarily, it shakes them to forgotten heights of energy and enthusiasm and leaves them nostalgically aware that by living elsewhere they may have renounced an essential part of their being. Under an objective guise I am, of course, pleading my own cause. Its effect upon the English is very different. It strips them of their joy in life, riddles them with rheumatism and wastes their gentler energies on mere survival.

I knew nothing of all this on that Sports Day in 1917, when I ran to join my parents and found them talking to what I saw as an elderly couple. Both our parents had come that day to see their children in their new surroundings, and very out-of-place those parents looked, my father with his unmistakably intellectual appearance, his crooked tie, his soft black hat worn a little to one side of his big scholarly head; my mother with her gentle, rather shy face and old-fashioned clothes, radiant to see us seemingly so at home in an atmosphere foreign to everything she herself had ever known, and rather annoying me by her radiance. I would have liked her to look more casual.

I stayed for a moment, answering these strangers' questions, but casting sideways glances towards what was going on in my new world, longing a little to escape and reintegrate the personality I was shy of donning in my parents' presence, but which was beginning to take shape. Then suddenly Mr. Mackintosh laid his hand on my shoulder and said: "Would you care to come and spend the summer with us at Samalaman?"

Struck, as it were by sudden joy, unhesitatingly I answered:

"Yes!" though I remember the dampening afterthought: would my father be able to pay for the journey? Otherwise I had no qualms. The mere name of "Samalaman" sounded in my ears like an incantation. I was not at all intimate at the time with any of the Mackintosh girls, but the prospect of trying my wings among strangers in a new environment, with no initiate from my home circle to drag me back to what they took to be my real self, was irresistible.

So it came about that I set out that summer with Mrs. Mackintosh and her three daughters for Samalaman House. We spent a night in Glasgow so as to catch an early train north. I remember quite clearly the long conversation I had with May that night, in the hotel bedroom, on the subject of sex and babies. I was not, at the time, particularly interested, and I was strangely ill-informed. It was a shock to me to discover that, in spite of her much stricter upbringing, May knew more than I did, and I can recall the flow of silent laughter that welled up inside me when it transpired that her source of information was the Bible, to which she had devoted much study.

The next day we took the train as far as Fort William, and from there another train to Loch Ailort, beyond which there was neither road nor rail. The Mackintosh motor-launch was waiting to carry us to Samalaman, by way of the three connecting sealochs that bite inland from the open sea beyond Samalaman Bay. In the motor-launch waited Johnnie and Angus, of whom I had already heard much from the three sisters. Johnnie, or Skipper Johnnie as they called him, captained the little craft. He was an elderly, weather-beaten man with white hair and a white moustache, blue eyes, under red eyelids puckered as though from scanning immense distances, and a face wrinkled with the dry humour of which I was soon to become a favourite butt. Angus, who acted as mechanic, was younger, and a fine figure of a man in the Scotch manner: tall, bulky and muscular with kindly blue eyes and a flowing dark moustache. He was that mythical figure, a Scotch peasant with a love of learning. He had taught himself Latin as well as mechanics, and he was said to take an interest in politics, which at the time seemed to count as an oddity. I took to them both at first sight with the passionate allegiance children so often devote to country people, with whose integrity contact is immediate and effortless.

And so we set out: Loch Ailort, Roshven Bay, Glenuig Bay. During the first of these I sat in the prow, with the wind and spray in my face. We were scarcely into the second but I was down under the deck, where I lay oblivious to sights of such beauty that even Dinnet was to pale by comparison: low purple hills, hollows where silver birches glimmer, stretches of sandy beach, some gold, one silver-white, occasional clusters of slate-roofed cottages with slow smoke rising from their chimneys, but on the whole few signs of habitation. I emerged only in time for my first sight of the islands of Rum, and of Eigg with its blue pointed hills, rising calm to westward out of an uncalm sea, and seeming within easy reach not only because Scotland is a small country where horizons never seem far distant, but because the humid quality of the light knits it all into close perspective. Looking back after over seventy years, that is the scene I find caught like a gleaming fish in the nets of memory.

We anchored in the lee of the little island that faces the landing-stage, and so, at last, reached Samalaman House. There my expectations were to be surpassed, for the house was full, and full especially of young people. Nor were these young people too young to interest me, hoping as I still did to meet my Sir Gervase Bellamy. There were Canadian connections of Mrs. Mackintosh, Rudolf and Cathy, a brother and sister, both in their late teens; there were the children, a daughter and two sons, of the Mackintosh brother who shared the estate with our hosts, Maisie, Alister and Charlie, aged twenty, eighteen and fourteen respectively; and there was a friend of Alister's, Erskine, aged seventeen, with the glamour about him of being on the point of entering the navy. On the adult level several guests, middle-aged by my standards.

As I said earlier, Mrs. Mackintosh had strict standards of behaviour, and this I soon discovered. A clear line was drawn between what was proper for little girls and what was permitted to all members of the male sex. "Boys will be boys!" was her maxim, and that covered the lot. But little girls, though they were not expected so much as to make their beds, were set to darn the linen for an hour or so in the early afternoon. Even this, though we grumbled a little among ourselves, was not without its charm. Not only did Mrs. Mackintosh read aloud to us as we darned, but I found a certain satisfaction in learning to do a beautiful darn on beautiful old table linen. What I did however resent was that the two older girls should be allowed the same freedom as the boys, no doubt because of their respective status, the one being a guest from overseas and the other part-owner of the house. Still, it rankled that they should have this advantage over us, and it was small comfort that Charlie would linger in the garden beyond the bay-window where we sat, making faces at us when his aunt's back was turned. Charlie did not interest me. He was only fourteen.

The rest of the time, day after day, was sheer joy. To begin with everything was new. Mrs. Mackintosh was nervous of many things. Boats were not her world, nor the sea, but she was completely at ease with dogs and horses, and for me the highlight of that summer was being taught the elements of riding, and that included saddling and grooming. Very soon, as soon as I had mastered the "trot levé", I was allowed to go off for a ride on my own, managing as best I could. Never shall I forget that ride, down half a mile or so of rough road, past the tiny hamlet of Glenuig (where the postwoman kept the stamps under her pillow), over the stream on the primitive wooden bridge, and into the woods and away.

My joy was so great that I chanted aloud verses from poems I knew by heart − they were legion − or sang whatever came into my head. When I turned at last to go home I was still in the same happy mood till we came, the pony and I, to the little bridge, and there, suddenly, he took fright and was off at a canter. Now, I had learned so far neither to canter nor to gallop and − though of this I was still unaware − I really only held onto the saddle by dint of careful balancing, not by any grip of the knees. It would have been difficult. I was only twelve years old and the pony was a stout one. Still, I held; but when we reached the road a trap was waiting for me. There was a cottage by the roadside where dwelled a woman reputed to have the evil eye. Just as we reached that cottage she emerged and, whether due to the evil eye or not, at her sudden appearance the pony shied, hesitated, and was off at a gallop. Tossed up and down like a pancake, I still clung, part to the saddle, part to the pony's mane, but humiliation was waiting for me round the first bend, in the shape of Skipper with his caustic blue eye. I knew he would put my lack of horsemanship down to the fact of my being "English", for Skipper was a tease, and the form his teasing took was to insist that, as there was no "Mac" before my name of Grierson, I must be English. "You'll be afraid, now", he would say, with his singsong West Highland accent. "You'll be afraid, being English, to take the boat out in the swell", which would put me on my mettle. Clinging still to the mane, somehow I made it to Samalaman House, and there an astonished Mrs. Mackintosh informed me that never, but never had the pony been persuaded to cross that bridge.

Another of the joys of Samalaman was having tea with Miss Maclean. A gentle little old lady, she was the last of that line of the Macleans. It was she that had sold the Samalaman house and property to the Mackintosh brothers when she could no longer cope with their upkeep, retiring herself to a cottage on the edge of Glenuig hamlet. There she lived alone with a small but lively person called Miss Baker, whom I was told was a trained nurse from Glasgow, though she did not dress for the part.

I took to them both as spontaneously as I had taken to Skipper and Angus. I was even to keep up a correspondence with Miss Baker in the years ahead, as being the only way to keep in touch with Miss Maclean. I was therefore doubly distressed when an unfortunate incident marred my first visit to the cottage.

The Mackintosh girls had told me all about Miss Maclean before we actually went to tea with her. One of the things they had told me was that a large box of chocolates was always ordered specially from Glasgow and produced when the three sisters came to tea. Children of large families, brought up in the austerity of war, are not indifferent to large boxes of chocolates; and I admit it was the sort of thing that figured high on my scale of values. On this occasion we had been invited without adult escort, but with recommendations to be on our best behaviour. Tea went off well, but as soon as that was over the air grew tense with expectation of what ritually was to come. Now the bane of childhood is that such a situation is exactly what may be counted on to bring on an attack of that wretched malady known as "the giggles". A child will glance at another child to see whether their thoughts are the same, and off they will go. What brought about our final undoing was that Miss Maclean, in her semi-blindness, opened the box upside down, causing a landslide. For a moment we sat with scarlet faces and streaming eyes, striving desperately to stifle our laughter, till the need to rescue the chocolates brought us to our senses. To this day it is a thing I hate to remember.

But where in all this was Sir Gervase Bellamy? Obviously absent, though no doubt I could have coined one out of Alister, as being of the right age, had he been of the same mind. But he was occupied with the Canadian girl, Cathy, whose brother, as I remember it, took no interest in me at all. There remained Erskine, who was friendly, and kindly enough to strike up something of a friendship with me. I accordingly set out to learn with him the things I now believed I must acquire if I was to rouse the interest of the other sex. They were the things that, in Britain and at that time, adolescent boys claimed no girl could do: bowl a ball overarm, throw a stone from the shoulder and throw it straight, catch a ball that is thrown straight at you, and above all, in the face of whatever challenge, seem fearless.

Fearless? As often as not, both in those days and at the present time, my courage has its best roots in a fear I have never quite conquered, the fear of ridicule.

I realize now that of all my summer at Samalaman brought me, what formed the strongest link between the Mackintoshes and me was, rather unexpectedly, music. Both Mr. and Mrs. Mackintosh were fond of music. Mrs. Mackintosh had some knowledge of it, while her husband had the immediate, instinctive response that makes playing a joy for the player. When they found I could sight-read the accompaniments to the "Songs of the North", which Maisie and Alister loved to sing on occasion, with everyone joining in, they began to encourage me to play. As I said earlier, music had tended to take a back place that first year in Edinburgh. At this uncritical encouragement all my dreams flared up again, and from that time onward the Mackintoshes gave me the thing most necessary to any player, however humble, an audience.

Nor was that all. Though I never visited Samalaman but three times in all, I carry it in me still. What is it that such sea- and landscapes do to us so to endear themselves that ever after they are an almost dolorous part of our inmost being? For years I believed these loves were atavistic and I used them as a loom on which to weave my own pattern of the romantic, slightly aggressive patriotism from which in Scotland we most of us suffer. Today I am not at all certain that atavism plays any part in it. When I first came to the Cévennes I suffered the same violence, and again when I went to Greece. I would like to believe there are affinities between landscapes and peo- ple. It would be flattering. But though I can enjoy flattery as well as most people, I prefer it to be credible. No; not affinities, nor yet heredity. Like great music and poetry, there are landscapes which give us a glimpse of a higher reality, and they leave us pregnant. Heredity may deal the cards, but the game is played by something else.

CHAPTER TWELVE

The Palais de Danse

And so at last, somewhere in the middle of it all there came the day, November the eleventh 1918, when our resilient world of youth seemed to have triumphed over the gloomy grown-up world. Armistice Day. As soon as the news was known our magnet drew us out to join our friends, and very soon Alice and her chief admirer had organized a bonfire and fireworks for the evening's celebrations, with the support of all the inhabitants of the three terraces. We children helped to gather all the dead wood we could find, blackening ourselves from head to foot with soot, and we piled it high, though the head-gardener looked askance at our preparations. He had long since discovered that our presence in Regent Terrace was a source of unaccustomed disorder, and he liked us not at all. But on that day of all days he could say nothing. I believe that even the most staid of our community, those that put their heavy feet down at any attempt to play tennis or miniature-golf on a Sunday, even they would have stood by us on Armistice Day.

That evening I remember as the highlight of happiness. Unforgettable because of what had gone before, and of what we now believed lay ahead of us: peace upon earth, goodwill towards men, the perennial hope of mankind. Experienced at my level, it was as though the new self I had felt stirring in me at school and at Samalaman came to life that November evening. I emerged from the aquarium on an uprush of emotion, a rocketing of happiness that burst aloft in a cascade of fiery flowers of which the night's fireworks were the visible sign. I was myself at last; or so it seemed to me. And indeed, something inside me had changed, or if not changed, then emerged. On the other hand none of our practical problems were solved, as soon grew evident, even at my level. Our money troubles, with the pound devalued and our income proportionately diminished, were worse than ever. Truly it was taking all the running our poor mother could do to stay on one spot. Her husband's situation required that she entertain his friends and colleagues, and an increasing number of distinguished men of letters. She did her best, but had neither money, strength nor courage left to entertain for her children, nor any experience to guide her. No attempt, consequently, was made to launch any of us on Edinburgh society, and by that I mean the West End.

Today what I ask myself is whether it would have been possible in the best of circumstances to launch us on any society. What prudent mother in those days, whether of sons or of daughters, would have welcomed to her fold five sisters whose poverty-hampered love of life expressed itself in homemade clothes of a flamboyant character as I shall tell - who were among the first in Scotland to adopt the mask of chalk-white face and scarlet lips then worn in Paris (I refer to Flora and Alice), who, taken all round, had enough of their mother's looks and their father's charm to make a stir, and who had not one brother to offset these disadvantages?

At this point it was the three youngest of us that were especially concerned. Molly was seldom at home, or so it seems to me on looking back. She had undermined her health doing war work both on the land and as a V.A.D; the young man she would have married had been killed; add to it all the strain of studying English under her own father and causing him immense embarrassment by being his best student, a thing he strove to disguise by hurrying over her name when hers was unavoidably the best essay, to give great praise to whoever came second. It was too much for her, and she would seize any occasion of going abroad or burying herself in the Episcopal convent in Aberdeen which is connected in my mind with St. Margaret's Episcopal Church where we used all to go on Sundays.

Flora, of course, was safe in Oxford. All we saw of her was when she came home on vacation, breathing a world unknown to me, playing and singing a new music whose strange idiom soon became a part of me, and speaking a language purged of inhibitions so much a part of me as to seem law. It was the beginning of the long struggle that was to follow, the struggle for truth, and which even today is not wholly resolved.

For Alice, Letty and myself the situation was far simpler than for Molly and Flora. After two and a half years of wartime Edinburgh, when pleasure of any sort must be wrested by our own effort from surrounding adult gloom, a burning will possessed us, the will to happiness. We believed, we really believed our troubles were over.

It was at this point that Letty and I went what I think of as underground in our search for excitement. We were of course sadly hampered by the exiguity of our pocket-money; but we had evolved two methods of getting round this problem. Our house was full of books, and although we had the good sense if not the honesty (we were never put to the test) never to pilfer a book from our father's library, where they lined three walls from floor to ceiling, we would occasionally select from a certain large bookcase on the top landing, where what might be called outcasts found their place, a few neat volumes, and raise the wind – the merest zephyr – by selling them.

Our other method led us into more dubious regions. We took to selling clandestinely what we could spare of our clothes. But first I must explain that the term "clothes" is perhaps a euphemism. Some, outgrown, had been made by our home-dressmaker, Miss Black or "Block" as we called her, a mediocre dressmaker but a delightful little woman in her forties, full of zest for life, who would entertain Alice – we only got the backwash – with accounts of an elderly suitor, invariably ending her stories with an abruptly virtuous: "Nothing sensual of course!" The rest consisted of "clothes" we had made ourselves. As I have already made clear, there was no money to spend on clothes for the youngest of us, who at the worst could always make themselves invisible by retiring into their school uniforms; but, undaunted, when a special occasion forced our hand we would buy, with what money our mother could afford to give us, a couple of yards each of some inexpensive but attractive material, usually one known as "government silk" which was printed in colourful gay designs, and out of this, a yard before and a yard behind, with shoulder-straps of velvet ribbon to give a little more length, and a narrow matching sash, we would evolve a dress, counting on our figures to do the rest.

Obviously the miracle was our finding someone willing to pay for such clothes; and they never made us rich. It was on a first floor in Leith Walk that we found such a buyer by following the instructions on a brass plate by the street door. Even today when in memory I climb those dreary stairs and breathe again the pervading smell, not so much of poverty as of some less definable ingredient; when in memory I ring the bell and the door is opened by a woman I now realize was probably a perforce retired prostitute, still painted and dyed, and we are ushered into her "parlour" – table in the middle with fruit under a glass globe, gloomy sideboard bearing artificial flowers – the same malaise grips me as then. As she examined what we brought (it was always Letty and I who shared these adventures) she would tell us tales of how her son was ruining himself on champagne suppers, conjuring up before our inexperienced eyes visions of riotous living which were hard to reconcile with the room we sat in. How old were we? Letty sixteen and I fourteen probably. It must have been shortly after the war ended. What did we do with our dubiously-gotten gains? On the proceeds of a couple of books we looked no higher than a chocolate hazelnut bar for each of us (they were massive at the time) or a banana-split at an Italian café in Leith Walk. Their enjoyment was slightly marred by a fear that, in what was then a disreputable part of the city, nothing, perhaps, was clean. But we were too deprived of food that tasted good to give free rein to our imaginations. We cast the thought aside.

The profits from our clothes led us into deeper waters. They allowed us, together with our weekly pocket-money, to make our secret way on an occasional Saturday afternoon to the Edinburgh Palais de Danse, a recent innovation and a sign of the times. We sometimes even managed to rise to a sixpenny Slow or Foxtrot with one of the professional dancers. These were grouped between dances in sort of pens – girls in one, young men in the other, and it was tremblingly we approached the men's pen to indicate which of them each of us wanted as a partner. We were both of us pretty expert dancers. We had been trained by one of Molly's admirers, a slightly crazy man who had been refused by the army but who danced like an angel. The rest of the time we sat at our little table spinning out through a straw the single glass of lemonade which was all we could afford, and watching out of the corner of an eye the young men who passed by our table to see if any of them looked promising . . . of what? Romance.

We were in love with love and believed we could meet it in the unlikeliest places. Inevitably we were invited to dance, and most of the young men were excellent dancers. It was when they opened their reticent Scotch lips that, at the accents which emerged, the vision of romance faded. We had Scotch accents ourselves, as we were to discover when at last we ventured over the border into England; but this was something different. The values we had absorbed at home were intellectual and cultural values. Somehow, we vaguely felt, this would never do.

One of our partners however danced so well, and promised by his own account to be so good a tennis player, that we invited him to the house. How we accounted for him to our parents I forget. We may have implied that we had met him in "the gardens".

He arrived exactly at tea-time and I shall never forget the occasion. Not only did our father chance to be at home, but a certain commander in the Royal Navy, another of Molly's admirers, had looked in for a game of tennis. The atmosphere was strained from the start, though our mother did her best, as she always did. Every time our "pick-up", as Letty and I called him to each other, opened his lips our father's face grew darker. Heaven knows he was no snob, unless the Scotch love of learning must count as snobbery; had the same young man had anything to say he would have been made welcome. As things were, our father may have been asking himself whether the "little wholesome neglect" I referred to earlier had not been carried too far.

After tea, on the tennis-court, the young man had his revenge. He was a far better player than any of us. But our relationship went no farther; and in their wisdom our parents asked no questions.

CHAPTER THIRTEEN

Studio Life

I must have been about fifteen when Alice began to accept me as a hanger-on in her art-college life. The life of an art student, all the world over, follows the same pattern of revolt against what we now call "bourgeois" standards, but then referred to as "philistine". I prefer the latter term; philistinism is not confined to the middle class, from which so many artists spring.

It was a disintegrating atmosphere for one as young as I was, and a far cry from our Edwardian nursery. As is clear, however, from my last chapter, we had strayed far from that nursery before ever I entered a studio. I found this new world warm and friendly and full of excitement.

Very soon I began to be asked to sit for my portrait by some of the post-graduate students, always on the look-out for a model. This gave me an entry to a number of studios besides the one Alice had persuaded her father to allow her to share with her new bosom-friend, Jessie. Looking back now, by the light of my children's and grandchildren's schooling in a French lycée, I ask myself how I managed to fit this new world into my school life. The fact is that, in contrast to the French lycée, and excepting on Tuesdays and Thursdays when there were Games (if I remember rightly), we were free after a late luncheon for the rest of the day. We were, of course, supposed to do our homework; but I was a past-master at postponing homework.

Jessie and Alice were equally well equipped to conquer their world. The difference was that where Alice owed her charm, apart from her looks, to a generous nature, and tremendous zest for life, Jessie's appeal was more deliberate, and more frankly sexual. They were, in fact, a tremendous pair, and a stream of art students flowed in and out of the studio where our parents presumed them so studious. After school, especially in the winter when our activities in "the gardens" were greatly reduced, I could seldom resist turning aside from my normal route home, to bask for an hour or so in their atmosphere, dreaming that some day I would live in a similar world where music would take the place of painting.

What our parents thought of it all I never knew. They were then so harassed by their financial difficulties and the stresses of our father's work at the university that they probably avoided thinking at all, except to hope for the best. Our mother was reassured, and perhaps a little flattered, that I should be in request as a model (there was, of course, no question of my posing in the nude, nor did she imagine there could be – nor did I, for that matter). It suggested a serious, hardworking context and justified my presence among the art students.

Even had they known, what to some extent they may have guessed, that very little real work was done in the studio, what could they have done? If my father had insisted that Alice renounce the studio and work at home, he could only have driven her to open revolt. Alice had gifts as an artist, but she had never then come under the sort of influence that could have canalized them and given them definite purpose. At the same time, we were all at the age when the biological urge is as powerful as, for our generation, it was ignorant. We were as though driven from within by a force which, as I said earlier, was given no outlet through a normal social life in those early Edinburgh years. I believe my mother was aware of all this, but having no solution at hand, so far as possible she closed her eyes to it. Like myself, she had a muddled way of shelving difficulties and hopefully leaving problems to solve themselves. I think, too, that she trusted in some fundamental quality she believed (hoped?) we must possess, which in the end would right the balance; and of course, in this case she was being set for the first time a problem of which she knew nothing. She herself had gone straight from an unnaturally prolonged nursery life into marriage. Her elder daughters had broken her in to the idea of a greater freedom than she had even dreamed could exist, but they had not yet challenged her standards of behaviour. Molly, when her young man was killed, took refuge in the adult world of grief; and when she emerged, her vital urge was temporarily broken. Flora had escaped to Oxford and flourished beyond the reach of family influence - and sometimes beyond college bounds, but of that we knew nothing. Alice was the first of our mother's children to force her out of her depths. Early in her married life a pro-fessor of psychology had advised her to "feed her children's crazes", and on this advice she had always acted to the best of her ability. But now here was Alice having cravings she had not the means or the experience to feed. She had even great difficulty in condoning them. She did at last venture on a word of counsel.

It happened at a time when Alice was hesitating between two of her admirers. One of them lived in Edinburgh, but the other had gone abroad for a year and was now expected home. Mother had been pondering the problem, and now tried to call up a little worldly wisdom. "Alice", she said at last, "Does F. kiss you?" "Yes!" replied Alice, somewhat taken aback. Such subjects had never been broached between them. There was a pause, during which Mother no doubt sat turning the matter over in her mind, for she hated to disappoint any of us. Taking courage, she went on in more determined tones: "Then you mustn't let C. kiss you!" "Oh!" cried Alice in dismay. There was another pause after which Mother gave her final pronouncement: "Well! You mustn't let them both kiss you!", and there she left it, while Alice escaped to rush upstairs and tell us "Mother's latest".

I may mention here that holding hands in a cinema, or an occasional kiss in a taxi, was as far as my imagination had strayed, and that, so far, I had experienced neither. Certainly we none of us drank a drop of alcohol, but danced the whole night through on fizzy lemonade. Nor did I ever see drink in any of the studios where I went, except, once, a bottle of inferior port wine, which we none of us touched. It was in the studio of an older artist who was painting my portrait at the time. He shared his premises with a pale friend, an indifferent artist but a man we liked for his gentle ways. They were, I believe, homosexuals, but at the time we had never heard that such a thing existed. We often went to see them because the two men gave us a safe feeling of unalloyed friendship with no disquieting undertones, and because the older man had a turn of mind that would touch off the springs of laughter in an irresistible way.

But if there was no drinking in what was now our world, whether in the private houses or the studios where we had our entry, there was a great deal of what was euphemistically called "sitting out". In organizing any sort of dance a lot of thought was spent on arranging suitable places: cushions would be put on stairs, or along passages. In buildings where there were several studios, an empty one would be left dark, and cushions put on whatever seemed a likely place to sit. Imagining as I did that kissing was as far as anyone went – and I knew very little about kissing – I was in perennial hope of meeting my true love and being drawn into amorous passages on a cushioned staircase; but conversely I was terrified of being lured into a dark room by the wrong man and being too polite to refuse.

Even at the dances Alice used to organize at home, and which are among my happiest memories, the same care was taken to provide for "sitting out" on cushioned stairs; but there were no dark rooms. But even so, how lucky we were to have parents whose vice was rather wishful thinking than over-anxiety.

These dances of Alice's took place twice a year, one big one during the Christmas holidays and a more informal and smaller one at Easter. As we asked nothing of our mother but to supply a buffet and a pianist, she was delighted there should be parties in the house, for whose success Alice took the whole responsibility. From Alice I learned once and for all, and have never forgotten, the basic rules that make for a good party. To begin with, only such girls were invited as met her standards of beauty or charm. She was not going to have it said that she feared competition; but even more, she wanted everyone to enjoy him or herself. Her next rule was that there must be three or four more men than girls. There were several reasons for this. First we had to take into account that our father was only too apt to lure down to his study any of the young men who interested him - unless we could persuade our mother to keep him out of the way. Then Alice had noticed that men were less inclined than girls to dance all through an evening. And of course, they receive more invitations than girls, or did in our time.

These dances cost us all a great deal of trouble. First we had to make lists of the people we wanted to invite. On one side were the girls that met Alice's exacting standards. On the other side of the page was a corresponding number of men, those we really wanted to come. We then drew up a second list headed "Spares", all of them men. From these we would choose replacements for those that were engaged elsewhere. That was all right. But there was another list involved, the list of the "Super Spares", those of our friends or acquaintances on whom we intended to fall back only in desperation, and in regard to this list a dreadful thing once happened. It haunts me to this day. One of these latter friends called and found us all out, but decided to wait for one of us to come home. He was put to wait in a room that had become my music-room, and there, on the grand pianoforte lay the lists, all three, in preparation for our Easter dance, and it was the name of this very man that headed the Super Spares.

We went through agonies of remorse, the more so that he was a man we liked and a good friend, but he was not our idea of a dancing partner. All we could do was to bury our heads in the hopeful belief that he had paid no attention to the lists.

CHAPTER FOURTEEN

To Have My Cake and Eat It

Certainly the atmosphere of first-year art-college life was a dissolving one for a schoolgirl of fifteen. It fed my dreams, but without harnessing them to any real effort. School began to take a back place, and I tended more and more to do only the minimum of work necessary to hold my own. As for music, with so much of my leisure spent in Alice's studio, although it remained the matter of my ambitions, I was neglecting the rigorous practice necessary to acquire technical mastery.

There were however more positive influences at work, though their effect was still only latent. In the morass of muddled thinking, into which my acquired beliefs and safe habits of mind seemed to be sinking, here and there the tip of a rock emerged on which I could later build, when distance gave perspective to it all.

To begin with, all through my childhood and early adult life there ran like a shining thread the visits of famous men. As soon as one of these visitors was expected, something in the air tautened, like an instrument tuned of a sudden to a higher pitch. It expressed itself in my mother's anxiety. Timid by nature, she had no notion what a halo of goodness she carried about her, or that it endeared her to everyone. On the other hand, she was acutely aware of her shortcomings as a housekeeper when it came to serious entertaining. Her stepmother's table had been no school at which to learn to give pleasure to such a palate as George Saintsbury's, famous connoisseur of food and wine, and, what was more, her husband's predecessor in the Edinburgh chair of English Literature. It had once happened when he was staying in the house, and guests were expected to dinner, that he had come down too early and found her alone in the drawing-room. She was so troubled at having to entertain him alone that she poured his "sherry" from the whisky decanter. Saintsbury sipped it thoughtfully, then murmured that though he found her sherry excellent, he would advise her not to serve it to the ladies when they arrived.

Some of these visits of great men I only knew as nursery legends: how Molly and Flora had been brought down from the nursery at W. B. Yeats' request, and how he had bowed low to Flora's three-year-old aloof dignity, and kissed her hand. It is pleasant to reflect that many years later they met again at the Longfords' in Ireland, and she so pleased him that he mentioned her in a letter to my father in the following terms: "... your daughter delighted me. She has charm and she has character so well blended that one did not know which was which. I would like her address, though indeed, seeing that I am more and more fixed here, apart from this American tour, it seems unlikely that we should meet".

Then there was the French poet, Angelier, who, so I was later told, fell on his knees at the sight of me at some very early age. This story did a great deal to bolster my self-confidence, and it badly needed bolstering in what was then the atmosphere on the nursery floor.

Both of these occasions were exceptions to the general rule of our being kept out of sight of guests, though by the time my turn came Molly and Flora were pretty free of the house. But Alice and Letty and I, imprisoned behind the little gate that topped the nursery staircase, had to steal our illegal share of whatever was going on. When there was a dinner party we knew that, when dinner was announced, the guests would file down from the drawing-room on the first floor, to the dining-room on the ground floor. This was the signal for us to hang over the top-floor banister, each with an undergarment in her hand, which we dropped on the heads of the last couple. Fortunately they were usually sure to be friends of the family. It was the sort of thing we found immensely funny.

The guests' return journey to the drawing-room was eagerly awaited for other reasons. It was the sign for us to draw on our long woollen stockings, rather than search for our bedroom slippers, but without troubling to put our feet in properly, so that they flapped ahead of us as we ran downstairs to devour what remains we could lay hands on in the dining-room. I remember our doing this once when Yeats was staying in the house. We thought our guests safe in the drawing-room. We were wrong. Yeats had gone down to our father's study to fetch a book of his poems he had been asked to read from. He emerged from the study when we were on our way upstairs, our hands and mouths stuffed with loot. We heard him mount the stairs behind us, laughing quietly to himself. We tried to hurry, but were hampered by our stockings, and had to run the gauntlet of his laughter till we left him behind by the drawing-room door. But all that was before we left Aberdeen.

I forget the names of most of the guests who slept in our fourposter bed; we met so few of them in those early years. But G. K. Chesterton I shall never forget. The second time he came we were children no more – I must have been seventeen – so we met as a matter of course. I remember how he came and joined us in our old schoolroom, by then my music room, and delighted us with Hilaire Belloc's *Cautionary Tales for Children*. From then on, when we would gather, as we were wont, for a séance of what we called, quite frankly, "being catty about about So-and-so" (and greatly enjoyed), scarcely had we finished with one victim and were about to turn to the next, when one of us would chant: "It was a very dreadful thing, and now we turn to Sarah Byng!"

I believe Chesterton was the happiest-looking grown-up I ever met, and no one could possibly feel shy with him. In spite of this, we had no great wish to go to his lecture. "Lecture" was a word we heard too often. Still, Letty and I were resigned; it was Alice who let us down. When after dinner Chesterton had gone to his room to prepare himself for the occasion, our mother, seeing no sign of her, called upstairs: "Alice! Are you coming to Mr. Chesterton's lecture?" To her unutterable dismay Alice's cheerful answer rang at once through the house: "Not bloody likely! I'm staying at home with a detective novel!"

A long chuckle came through Chesterton's half-open door. His sympathies were with Alice.

We drove to the lecture (without Alice) in a horse-cab, though how that could be in the early 'twenties surprises me. No doubt our mother still had her prejudices. The fact has stuck in my memory because Chesterton insisted upon lowering his immense weight as nearly as possible in the exact middle of the vehicle, out of consideration for the horse.

In spite of these early encounters with our father's guests, the general rule was that we be kept out of sight. Even after we had outgrown the nursery and unavoidably met them, at breakfast and so on, it never occurred to us to join in the conversation, or volunteer a remark. It was as though our father, extending his native modesty to include us, was so certain we would say the wrong thing if given a chance, that he cast a sort of spell over us that kept us silent. Indeed he so paralysed me intellectually that, though I loved him dearly, I believe I never expressed a personal opinion in front of him till long after I had left home.

For all these reasons, I was at a loss the day one of our father's poets, a man of a younger generation than most of our visitors, broke the unwritten rule and tried to bridge the gulf. It occurred in the same year as Chesterton's visit; I remember that my mother was a little distressed because this Poet had written to say he would arrive only just in time for dinner. As the lecture was to be immediately after dinner she feared a rush, a thing that made her nervous. She asked me to receive him in her place, show him his room, and ask him to hurry, thus leaving her time to dress in peace.

I went about my preparations early, in my usual leisurely manner, taking time to wash my hair and polish my nails. For once I had a really beautiful dress which Alice had handed on to me. It was of quite simple cut, but of sumptuous material, shot silk of deep greens and blues. It had a broad sash and a skirt that was full, but not too full: its real beauty was in the material. I had never yet been to a hairdresser, but Alice had cut my hair shoulder-length. Never having had a permanent wave, I simply dried my dripping hair upside-down before a gas fire to give it volume. The odd thing is that I had no idea what sort of man our guest would prove to be, and had no personal interest in him. It was all part of a discipline which, under the influence of Elinor Glyn (does anyone read her today?), we imposed upon ourselves. It required that we never allow ourselves to slack off, but strive, whatever the effort, always to look our best. Alice and Letty had read Elinor Glyn; I had not. But they had conveyed to me the purpose of it all, which was to keep alive, after marriage and beyond it and for-ever, the early tremors of romance. And so I had grafted this new technique of approach onto the earlier one, with which I had hoped to capture a Sir Gervase Bellamy. It was no longer a training of eye and arm, with a view to seducing the loved one on what I took for his own ground. I had grown wiser.

All this being so, I felt a little shy when our guest arrived. I did as my mother had bade me, took him to his room and asked him to change quickly as it was nearly dinner-time. He seemed as shy as I was, and we exchanged few words.

Now, my mother had one delightful quality. She could never resist handing on a compliment to whichever of her daughters it concerned. At the same time, she felt she probably ought not to do so. It was accordingly with a rather guilty little giggle that she told me the next day how our guest had confided in her that he thought me so beautiful he could think of nothing else while I was in the room. I was staggered. I was naturally also delighted. But especially I was staggered. It was a totally new situation and I had no idea how to deal with it. So far, I had at least been natural, if silent, with our distinguished visitors; they counted not a whit, as far as I was concerned, as human beings. They were famous names. Now I became so self-conscious I could barely breathe. Fortunately he had to leave the next day.

About a year later there was a sequel to this event. I was called to the telephone. Someone wanted to speak to "Professor Grierson's youngest daughter". It was my poet, on a flying visit to Edinburgh. I at once told him how sorry I was that my father was away from home. "But it isn't your father", said the voice at the other end of the line, "It's you I want to see." Panic-stricken, I told him he could come to tea that day. I would have done better to invent some excuse. To begin with, I had a terrible cold in the head. What was more, I had at last gone to the hairdresser. I had my hair "shingled", and it had been badly done. When the young man (relatively young) arrived, I took him to my father's study, where my mother and some other people – I forget who – were having tea, and for the rest of his visit I sat blowing my nose and speaking only when there was no escape. I never saw him again. I do not even remember his name.

It was a far cry from Yeats and Chesterton to our studio cronies, with whom I was much more at ease. But here too there were hierarchies. There were some genuinely talented elements among the post-graduate students, but they were of an older generation, and beyond our immediate circle. Their preoccupation was with art; ours with the "vie bohème". Before, however, the water of Bohemia had quite closed over our heads, we were lucky enough to be admitted, Letty and I as usual in the wake of Alice, to a more adult level of studio life. A gifted painter, Eric, whose wife, Cecile, was herself an artist of talent, and the daughter of an Edinburgh painter, kept open house in their studio on Friday evenings. We were made free of these occasions, and could drop in any Friday after dinner, to drink a cup of coffee and spend the evening among their friends.

At the time I am writing of, it was thwarting for an artist to be confined to Edinburgh. Glasgow had its tradition of painting and architecture, its link with Vienna, and a better-educated public. In Edinburgh a painter of talent might emerge, perhaps, more easily than he would have done in Glasgow, but something would be lacking. I am incompetent to say what. The temptation for the less stable was to settle down within the limits of local repute, risking an early frost, and drown in talk and drink the haunting sense of unfulfilment.

In the case of Eric and Cecile, a sort of equilibrium seemed to have been struck: the one more gifted and more fragile, the other more intellectual and better balanced. The interest of the evenings varied, but for me they were always interesting. For the first time I was hearing serious conversation about art,

or what I took for such, and though I was too ignorant to follow it, it made me feel grown-up. Sometimes there would
only be five or six people present. On other occasions a crowd
would have gathered, because some eminent visitor was
expected, or some beautiful, sophisticated woman whose portrait Eric happened to be painting. The talk was, as I said,
beyond my scope, and not one of the people I met there was
to play an important part in my life, but I found the atmosphere intoxicating, as though from this threshold I gained a
clearer vision of what my own life could hold for me.

The truth is that at about this time I had become aware of a
split in my inner equilibrium. Within me surged a fund of
dynamic energy, seeking an outlet. I felt it as a thirst for life,
for excitement, for fame, for success with men, for distant
horizons, for all my hands had never touched or my eyes seen.
I remember one Spring evening, as I prepared unwillingly for
bed, how I stood for a moment, gazing out of my bedroom
window at the shadowy gardens beyond, and all my inner turmoil condensed and simplified into a primitive longing to be
out and away, like the witches of old, to dance on the new
grass by the light of the moon.

And, seemingly in opposition to all this, there was the
thought of marriage. In the depths of my heart, I wanted that,
too. The trouble was that I wanted everything, but because I
was a girl, I believed I must choose.

It was the either-or attitude that was in the air when I was a
child which did the harm. As soon as I began to dream of a
career, I was faced with what seemed to follow as surely as
night follows day, the having to renounce all idea of marriage.
I would loudly proclaim my intention never to marry, but my
mother had only to say, in a half-hearted attempt to go with
the times: "Well if you don't marry you will always be able to
do this or that", for my heart to sink, the more so that it was

never anything very exciting she suggested. Renouncing marriage to me meant renouncing love. No more, no less. Ours was a world where illegitimate babies were as unthinkable as they were presumed, in certain circumstances, inevitable; and virginity as essential to "winning a good man's love" as was once a dowry. That was all that had filtered through to us of a code of behaviour so old, its true purpose had faded out.

I am not taking into account here the Christian institution of marriage. It has an extra dimension which alters the whole situation. I am referring to something more universal and much older. Its purpose may well have been to protect and shelter the rising generation, and not, as we women are apt to assume, to "grind down the face" of the weaker sex.

I was aware of none of this, but only of the split, a split whose symbol I now see in the image of the virgin and child, the virgin, the woman's masculine, personal and intellectual side, the mother her visionary and maternal, upon which the future of the world depends. But: "It's certain there is no fine thing since Adam's fall but needs much labouring". We are now being given the chance of exchanging that labour for one with time off and more immediate. returns; perhaps at the risk of the future.

As I said, I knew nothing of all this; but there was one thing I was quite clear about: I had neither the temperament nor the courage to fly in the face of middle-class convention and compromise. It was a bleak outlook.

But now here was Cecile, achieving under my very nose the synthesis I believed impossible. Here she was, married and with two children, and if not as good a painter as her husband, yet equally respected, and having a style of her own which owed nothing to him. It was beginning to look as though I might be able, after all, to have my cake and eat it.

CHAPTER FIFTEEN

André Raffalovich

Oddly enough, it never occurred to me that my success as a pianist was going to depend to a very great extent upon the amount of work I was prepared to do. Perhaps I was too Scotch to waste good effort on what might prove abortive. Moreover, I was always apt to put the cart before the horse. At the time, the only thing I really put my mind to was the essays I had to write for our English teacher; but for me that did not count as work, because I enjoyed it as much as long ago I had enjoyed making sand castles. This was a sign I might have followed up, but if there was one thing on which I was determined, it was that I would not study English Literature under my father at the university.

I was at this stage when a new door opened to us. It opened onto a very different world from any we had hitherto known, that of André Raffalovich, a wealthy man of Russian Jewish origin, a convert to Catholicism, and a great connoisseur of the arts. He had settled in Edinburgh in the wake of his great friend, John Gray, and his chief occupation was entertaining. My parents were the first of us to be invited to his house, but little by little he came to include us all, inviting us separately, which was sensible of him.

Under the title of *Two Friends*, a book on André Raffalovich and John Gray was published privately some years ago. It taught me a great deal of their history, and made me realize that, apart from my personal impressions, all I really knew about them was their legend, and like most legends it fitted, not necessarily the facts, but some more intangible thing, perhaps their essence. It is this legend, bathed in my own impressions, still very distinct, which I shall try to recount. I shall correct, where honesty requires, what I now know to be inept.

The Raffalovich family came originally from Odessa, where André's father and uncle were bankers, and both of them true followers of the Jewish faith. When, in I do not know what year, a law was passed in Russia to the effect that all Jews must convert to Orthodox Christianity or emigrate from Russia, of the two brothers one, the uncle, renounced Judaism and remained in Odessa, while André's father kept his faith and emigrated to France. "It is a very moral story", remarked old Miss Gribbel, who told me all this (an old friend of André's mother, she had kept house for him ever since he left Oxford), and there was a twinkle in her wicked eye. It was indeed a moral story; for the uncle who remained behind was shortly ruined, whereas the father settled in Paris and prospered as a banker. He was married by this time to a niece to whom, for reasons of family finance, he had been betrothed when she was still in her cradle. She had grown into a beautiful and cultured woman, had borne her husband three children, of whom André was the third, and then announced that she had done her duty by him, and intended henceforth to live the life that interested her. She divided her time between study (by the time of her death she apparently spoke eight languages fluently, and was studying Arabic) and entertaining in the family *hôtel particulier*, where my father-in-law told me his father once dined. Miss Gribbel knew the house well, having lived there for a number of years as companion to Madame Raffalovich. She told me the dining-room was as vast as a chapel but that when guests were staying the children were put to sleep on the stairs (this I took as a manner of speaking). To all this Miss Gribbel added that the beautiful Madame Raffalovich found her son André's ugliness so distressing that, as soon as might be, she sent him to finish his studies in Oxford, eventually settled him in London, and asked her friend and companion to join him there and keep house for him, and entertain his friends. Which she did.

In London, with Miss Gribbel as hostess, André began the entertaining he was to keep up all his life. He also wrote poetry, rather decadent poetry, the legend said, of which he published several volumes. Those were the days when Oscar Wilde was at the height of his literary and social success. I believe he once referred to Raffalovich as "the Russian who keeps not a salon but a saloon". Certainly Raffalovich was no intellectual snob; the people he invited were the people who interested him.

It was during those London years that André met John Gray, then a clerk in the Foreign Office, but also one of the most promising of the younger poets of the time, and an exceptionally beautiful young man. Their friendship was to last till they died within a few months of each other in 1934. I later learned (but not from Miss Gribbel) that rumour made of John Gray the original of Wilde's Dorian Gray. There was apparently a lawsuit about it, which Gray won, but the belief that, at least as regards looks he was indeed Wilde's model, still subsisted when I left Edinburgh.

The story of the two friends' conversion to Catholicism as told me by Miss Gribbel is a curious one, and apparently not at all true. It is mentioned in the book I referred to as having W. B. Yeats as its source, which surprised me, because I most certainly got it from Miss Gribbel. Her story was that the two friends went cruising on the Mediterranean in a black yacht named the *Iniquity*. During their cruise they chanced to put in at a little Italian port where some religious festival was in full swing, and they both underwent a sudden conversion to the Catholic faith. On their return to England, so went the story, John Gray decided to take orders, and went and studied at the Scotch College in Rome. After his ordination he was appointed to a parish in Edinburgh, actually in the Cowgate, one of the roughest slums in the city, where he worked with courage and abnegation. (Wicked Miss Gribbel maintained that the ecclesiastical authorities sent him to Scotland because he was too well-known elsewhere.)

The part of the story which is especially open to query is the cruise on board the *Iniquity*, and Gray's conversion was apparently a longer affair than the legend suggests. As regards André Raffalovich, I know no more than the legend.

When I first came to know the three friends, André Raffalovich, John Gray and Miss Truscott Gribbel, to give her her full title, they had lived for many years in Edinburgh, André having followed his friend north. A new church had been built with generous contributions from Raffalovich and Sir Robert Lorimer as architect, and Father Gray had been appointed as its first parish priest. André attended Mass daily, going there, as he went everywhere, in a taxicab, which he kept waiting at the door; and he gave generously to the Church. The rest of his time he spent entertaining the intellectual and artistic élite of Edinburgh (so, having been a frequent guest, I like to believe) and a number of literary and ecclesiastical visitors.

Before I tell what I knew of him at first hand, I must give one more story from Miss Gribbel's delightful repertoire. It concerns not André himself but his sister. According to the story, when O'Brien, the Irish nationalist leader, was imprisoned by the English, a rumour went about Paris that he was deprived of the most necessary articles, and had no clean linen to change into. When this rumour reached her, Sophie Raffalovich went straight out and bought twelve pairs of silk pyjamas which she sent to O'Brien in his prison. The Irishman was so touched that the moment he was set free he went over to Paris, called at the Raffalovich house, fell on his knees at Sophie's feet, and asked for her hand in marriage. They married, and at the time Miss Gribbel told me the story they were living, so she said, peacefully in the south of England, doing endless good about them, pillars, both of them, of the Catholic Church.

To return to Edinburgh, André's entertaining followed a regular cycle: a luncheon party on Sunday, a tea-party on Saturday afternoon, and a more exclusive dinner party on Tuesday evening. From this cycle he never to my knowledge departed till the day he died. Edinburgh society was divided between those that were invited to his house, and accepted with alacrity, and those who were not invited, and took refuge in mild disapproval. Anti-semitism would be too strong a word.

Nine Whitehouse Terrace, where Raffalovich lived, was a pleasant sunny house, set in a garden full of lawns and roses. Those roses were André's pride, and I remember how displeased he was when a certain Major, mellow from the luncheon champagne, plucked one and gave it to my sister Letty. Nothing was said, but much was expressed by the sudden freezing of André's features.

The house was soberly furnished in the English taste; but here and them, on shining polished table, or on mantelpiece, contrasting objects of faint decadent beauty were laid out, and changed from week to week: a book of poems bound in some unexpected colour and material; some little thing which for reasons peculiar to himself had drawn Raffalovich's birdlike eye, and delighted him by its sheer gratuity; or flowers arranged with sparing, consummate art. They betrayed his natural taste; but what he professed was a love for the simple, healthy things of life. Even as he invited you to admire a slim volume of modern verse, specially bound for him in fuchsia silk, "Dear child", he would murmur, "when the time comes for you to use perfume do, do, avoid the synthetic scents and confine yourself to real flower extracts", or, when I appeared before him for the first time with powdered face and scarlet lips: "Such a pity, don't you think, that Lady Margaret So-and-So makes her face up?" In much the same spirit he provided me across the years with a perfect lore of what he deemed items of practical advice, for which I never found any application when later faced with my own domestic problems. When I became engaged, his word of counsel was: "Never give your poor husband heated-up remains. Re-heating caus-es a chemical change in food that makes it fatal to the digestion!" How was I to reconcile this with the chapter in my new French cookery book on, "L'art d'accommoder les restes"? Another time, when I admired some roses in a vase, he said: "Do you know how I preserve my cut roses?" and waited for an answer with his delightfully ugly head on one side. "Do you put aspirin in their water?" I innocently enquired. "Aspirin!" he recoiled in horror, as though I had suggested he gave his roses morphia injections, or revived them with LSD. "Aspirin! no! my secret is that I never change their water." It never worked with me; I think his secret was simply that his roses came straight from the garden, and not from a florist's shop.

The prevalent atmosphere in Raffy's (as, behind his back, he inevitably came to be called) house was, in fact, *fin de siècle*: Huysman, with whom he had corresponded, superimposed upon a classic English background. The flowering of his true nature had here been pruned to fit the setting of his deliberate choice. It was really all very delightful, and quite unlike anywhere else. The moment you reached the drawing-room, breathless, in my case, lest I be late – a thing he could not tolerate, making clear his displeasure without a word uttered – he would be at the door to greet you. Drawing you in, he would lead you to the guest who was to sit next to you at table, and then stand aside, with a watchful look, his head on one side, waiting for you to start striking sparks off one another. Nothing was so certain to paralyse me. I remember how once, when for a moment I stood tongue-tied, he vanished from the room leaving us where we were. He was soon back to "rescue me", so he believed, from the guest, with whom I was now on excellent terms. Drawing me aside he whispered in reassuring tones: "I saw you didn't like Mr. So-and-So, so I went down and changed your place at table. I put you next to Father Gray".

It may have been to Father Gray that I owed my early inclusion in Raffalovich's circle. Certainly I was one of the only two people in their early 'teens that ever to my knowledge entered the sanctuary (the other was Harry Lintott, who later rose very high in the Civil Service), and my first invitation occurred shortly after I had met Father Gray in our own drawing-room. Father, or Canon Gray as he was shortly to become, was fond of children and can have had no idea how much he terrified me. His close-cropped dark hair fitted his head like a skull-cap and under it his full, rather highly-coloured face was set in an expression of what looked like self-satisfied irony. I must have been about fourteen when he first called on my parents, and espied me sitting reading in a corner of the room. As soon as possible he came across to where I sat and enquired what book I had been reading. Shyly I handed him Walter de la Mare's *Peacock Pie*. In a sudden spurt of confidence I even showed him the poems I best liked. He read them through and the ironic expression on his face altered no whit. I froze at his seeming lack of understanding, and from then on would have as little to do with him as possible.

My mother afterwards discovered and explained to me the origin of his disconcerting expression. He had apparently at one time had facial paralysis, and it had permanently affected the mobility of his facial muscles. Remorse gnawed at my vitals, but the uneasiness persisted. Actually it had another cause, for Canon Gray had an elegance of speech that was part old-fashioned and part of deliberate choice. For example, he would address me as "little maid" which curled me up like a hedgehog. When once he suggested to my mother that I spend an afternoon with him at the Edinburgh Zoological Gardens, of which he was, I believe, a "Founder", I beseeched her to invent some likely excuse; an afternoon alone with Canon Gray was something I felt I could never face. If I knew anything of my mother, she probably let the cat out of the bag by inventing far too many excuses.

Later I came to a better appreciation of Canon Gray, but I never quite got over my shyness of him. My link with the two friends lasted till their death within a few months of each other. Nine Whitehouse Terrace provided me with the only social training I ever received, till I went to Vienna and fell under the influence of old Clara Wittgenstein, the aunt of Wittgenstein the philosopher, to whom Donald Tovey introduced me. But Vienna is another story.

To this day I am deeply grateful to Nine Whitehouse Terrace. If at home, when important guests came, we were tacitly expected to remain silent, there we must talk, or take the consequences. There, too, we met as many writers as at home; but they were not the same writers. Those I best remember are Compton Mackenzie and E. M. Forster.

In point of fact, it was not so much the people we met at Nine Whitehouse Terrace that was important in the long run, it was the windows the two men opened up for us on a world very different from our father's, and encouraged us to explore. It was Canon Gray who introduced me to the poetry of Francis Jammes, and Raffalovich who gave me my first volume of Arthur Waley's translations from the Chinese. It was Raffalovich who sang me the praises of Vita Sackville-West's long poem, *The Land*, newly published; from him I first heard of Proust, and of Julian Green.

To this day I preserve, carefully wrapped in tissue paper, the two exquisite little silver toast-racks which were Canon Gray's wedding present to me. I have never been able to use them. No French bread could ever be squeezed into such tiny stays. But occasionally I would take them out and polish them, and sigh that life's opportunities should be so infinitely richer than our powers of assimilation. But though I was too young, and too callow, to profit as I might have done by the contact of these two remarkable men, some cultural residue remained to me, and some elements of social usage with which to face adult life.

Miss Gribbel was the first of the three friends to die, as was normal, for she was very much their senior. She died at the age of eighty-seven. After a brief period of mourning, the parties went on as before, except that one was no longer drawn onto the sofa to listen to the old lady's whispered racy talk, while "Raffy" watched from a distance with an unquiet eye. André died four years later, and Canon Gray, as I said, a few months afterwards. By that time, I was married and had been living in France for four years. During those years, I had seen them every time I was home on a visit to my parents. When the news of their death reached me, my very real sorrow was slightly, well, not alleviated, but shall I say disturbed, by what struck me as an element of delightful irony; for I learned, almost at once, or so it seems to me on looking back, that Nine Whitehouse Terrace had been acquired by the new Professor of Theology. I could only hope that no breath of disrespect for the Pope, no sweeping condemnation of Rome, would ruffle the peace of the house. I hoped, too, that the two friends' gentle ghosts would see the joke.

CHAPTER SIXTEEN

Donald Francis Tovey

Though I began going to André Raffalovich's house when I was fourteen or fifteen, it was not till I was seventeen that I was invited with any regularity, and not until I had spent my first year in Vienna that I was admitted to the Tuesday evening dinners. By that time I had come under other influences. Raffalovich's was in any case rather a civilising than a kindling force. The stimulus required to galvanise my native laziness, and my tendency to dream rather than act, I got from other sources, so far as I got it at all.

The earliest of these influences was undoubtedly my sister Flora. The long vacation periods brought her home from Oxford, trailing in her wake new sources of emotion. At her touch, star after star lit up in my firmament, names all new to me, but some very old: Plato, Herodotus, Saint Augustine, Thucydides (she was reading Greats), and then a great leap to contemporaries I knew as little of: Aldous Huxley, a mysterious Lady Ottoline Morrell, Lytton Strachey, Aubrey Beardsley (who had been a protégé of Raffalovich's); I cite at random. She brought, moreover, with her, songs by Fauré, Duparc and Debussy, and sang them in her slight but true soprano, accompanying herself with delicate, hesitant, undeveloped hands; for she had never studied the pianoforte, and only briefly the violin. I remember what joy it was when I grew accustomed to Debussy's idiom, at first too strange to me for pleasure, and came to delight in his haunting, two-dimensional world, whose power is especially evocative, and whose depths depend, perhaps, upon the extent to which the listener is attuned to his cultural background. It was probably the synthetic charm of the "Bilitis" songs that first roused my interest in Greece. Hearing the songs by chance, years later, was a bitter experience. My critical sense forced me to admit that they are among Debussy's weaker works, but their hold on me was as powerful as ever, for they conjured up, untarnished, the long spring evenings when, drunk with Flora's talk and her singing, I would wander about the gardens, feeling as though imprisoned under grey skies that pressed upon my spirits and seemed to offer no escape. The only exotic splash of colour, the glowing yellow laburnum, was soot-besmirched and scentless, as I discovered all too soon.

Flora opened other doors. She gave me my first notions of elegance. On a tiny dress-allowance she achieved a miracle. She had not only, as I mentioned earlier, shed her spectacles and her stays; she had natural poise, and she gave point to the simplicity imposed by poverty by concentrating on such details as shoes. Her shoes were high-heeled – it was the fashion – but they were of the first quality. And finally, although the permanent wave had not yet been invented, she had learned to curl her hair with hot tongs in such a way as to form a halo round her face – many young people do the same today, some of them men – giving full value to the lovely bone-structure of her face. She who had been considered plain in her childhood was now, in her own way, beautiful.

No doubt Flora's influence was the greater on me that she never sought to influence. She was already hostile to religion (but I realise now that by "religion" she meant something different from what the word means to me, today), yet she would answer my questions on the subject precisely, never

stirring up the wider issues beyond my immediate require-
ments; nor did she make any attempt to undermine my beliefs.
Hers was even then a clear, objective mind, respectful of other
people's mental privacy. I trusted her absolutely.

But even Flora never quite screwed me up to the point of
action. In practice she inclined as I did to believe one could
owe the fulfilment of one's dreams to the toss of a dice. She
was no great worker. It was my pianoforte teacher, Miss
Maclachlan, who brought me at last to realise that my future
was a thing I must forge for myself. She had studied music in
her youth in Stuttgart, and the memory of those enchanted
years still nourished her. She understood at once my longing
to go abroad, and approved my choice of Vienna, though she
knew no more than I did who was then the best teacher, nor
whether he would be likely to accept me as a pupil. She was
always perfectly honest about my shortcomings: I was no
infant phenomenon, a fact I could hardly bear to face, and I
had come late to the notion of real work. She admitted that I
was gifted, and she had the good sense to close no doors by
killing hope, saying that no one could tell how I might yet
develop, and adding that if I failed to make the concert standard as a soloist, I could form a chamber music group and still
hope to make music the matter of my life. It was as much, at
that stage, as I hoped for. She knew me better in some ways
than did my mother: she never suggested I might teach. The
gift for teaching is one of the rarest of all, and one of the most
important. My father had it, but I had not.

Over and above my weekly lessons with Miss Maclachlan I
used to go and spend most Sunday mornings with her. She
would regale me with coffee and cakes and talk of her student
days in Stuttgart, and she would allow me to play on the
beautiful grand Steinway pianoforte she had recently bought
with her savings, and on which her pupils were rarely allowed

to perform. When I was about sixteen she also gave me some excellent advice which I was able to follow. She suggested that as I must continue school, but should already be studying such branches of music as harmony and counterpoint, I might attend some of the music classes organized under the auspices of the Workers' Educational Association which were held on certain evenings in the music classrooms of the University. She added that I could in the same context follow the Musical Interpretation Classes held by the great musician who was then at the head of the Musical Faculty: Donald Francis Tovey.

I had already had fleeting glimpses of Tovey when he dined at our house, and I had heard him play. I have written elsewhere about his playing. I shall confine myself here to quoting what three of his contemporaries have said of him; their opinion will have greater weight than mine.

In a book of conversations with Pablo Casals, written by a Spanish journalist whose name I forget, Casals, who often played Tovey's works, places him among the "three great unrecognized musicians" of our time, and winds up his moving account of his friend with the words: "Tovey a été l'un des plus grands musiciens de tous les temps".

I think it was in 1958, nineteen years after Tovey's death, that Albert Schweitzer came to Paris to be received into the French Académie. Though my acquaintance with him was slight - I had met him in the 'thirties in Tovey's and in my father's drawing-rooms — I went and called on him in his hotel, driven by a longing to touch again one of the links that bound me still to Tovey. I found flocks of Schweitzer's friends and admirers waiting for a moment's conversation with him. I suggested to his secretary, who had already announced me (adding a reference to Tovey, without which I felt he might easily have forgotten who I was), that I thought it would be

kinder in me to leave without seeing the great man, so slight
was my claim. But the secretary said: no; that Dr. Schweitzer
was anxious to see me so that he could talk once more about
his friend.

I waited nearly three hours, during which time the secretary
came several times to ask me not to leave. When at last my
turn came to sit side by side with Dr. Schweitzer on the narrow iron bed in the room of the little Left Bank hotel where
he was staying, his eyes filled with tears at the mere sound of
Tovey's name.

And once, much earlier, when I was a young married
woman, my husband and I took the train from Metz, where
we were then living, to Luxembourg, to hear the recital
Edwin Fischer was giving in that town. By chance on our way
home we were in the same compartment as Fischer and we
got into conversation. When he learned that I had been a
pupil of Tovey's he told me that he had met him once only,
in 1913, but that he had never forgotten him. When we left
the train at Metz he gave me his calling card and asked us to
come and see him if ever we came to Berlin. Tovey's name
had acted as an open sesame.

I quote the opinions of these three musicians because they
are of greater weight than mine. Nothing, not even a gramophone record, remains – except possibly one of Adila Fachiri
and Tovey playing sonatas – to allow those who were told
that Tovey was above all an erudite, to discover that he had
the technical mastery of a virtuoso and the magical insight of
a composer. Nothing. Unless an echo still haunts the quiet
places of our house in Regent Terrace. No doubt it is pre-
sumptuous of me to believe that only our house could serve as
a shell to capture his lost music; he played in so many places.
I doubt whether in any of them he roused quite such emotion
as in my adolescent heart and mind, or telescoped for any

other ignorant fool the anguished joy of initiation within the limitless limits of a late Beethoven sonata.

I went to Tovey's Interpretation classes, as I did to the Harmony and Counterpoint classes held by Dr. Petrie Dunn, one of Edinburgh's most esteemed pianoforte teachers. I sat at Tovey's feet (in a manner of speaking) and listened in ecstasy while he played. Breathless I strove to follow his verbal wanderings through the workshops of great music, as he sought to explain to us in words – never for him an easy manner of expression – by what means and with what precise tools emotion may be translated into the language of music.

There followed for me an exciting period. Anxious not to lose a word of what Tovey said and, to be perfectly honest, hoping to capture his attention though not really expecting to do so, I sat as near the front of the classroom as I dared. Soon it seemed to me that at the key moments of whatever he was playing – fortunately he gave frequent illustrations of what he was trying to explain – his wide-apart eyes would for a second flash in my direction as though to gauge whether or not I had got the point, and by doing so help me to get it. I told myself I was imagining things, but soon realized I was not. Then there came a day when I persuaded my father to write and ask Tovey's advice about my ultimately going to study music in Vienna, and with whom. He gave me the letter to take with me to the music classrooms, telling me to give it to the janitor, and adding that Tovey would probably see me after the class. I did as he bade me, but I was so afraid this gesture would be recognized for what, in fact, it was – an attempt to wile my way into Tovey's magic circle – that I fled home as soon as the last notes had sounded. The following week he set my heart wildly beating by calling out, just as he was leaving the platform at the end of the class: "Oh Miss Grierson! will you wait for me? You ran away so quickly last week that I couldn't catch you".

And so it came about that evening, and on many more, that he saw me home. Through the gloom of wintry Edinburgh we walked, over the North Bridge (or was it the George the Fourth? My memory for names is fading), down past the North British Hotel and past the General Post Office, round and up Regent Road between the Royal High School, where Walter Scott was a pupil, and the Calton Jail, which then stood where the Government Buildings stand today. I had always a moment of hopeful anguish when we reached the General Post Office. Tovey had not yet come to live in Royal Terrace, round the corner from us. His house was then in George Square, on the far side of the university. I told myself that if he came so far as to accompany me up Regent Road, then really he must be taking me seriously, which was all I asked. He was twenty-nine years my senior, and I never thought of him otherwise than as an object of distant veneration. My feeling for him never even lessened my interest in younger men. What it did was to guide my instinct towards love into the same watercourse as my ambitions, and protect me to some extent against the dispersion which had confused my earlier adolescence. It also gave me moments of such joy that I would suddenly fall silent in a room full of chattering people, isolated from them by a barrier of happiness so palpable, it seemed it must be visible as a ring of fire. But that was later.

I never met Tovey in the spring or summer. He left always early in March, when the musical academic year ended, for England, or on concert tours in Germany or the United States. It is the dark November evenings when the mist sets a halo round the city lamps, and their reflection scintillates on greasy pavements, that remain to me now of my Edinburgh youth, as Vienna has left me the unearthly green of the Karlskirche's dome against the midnight summer sky.

Emotion lifts its context out of time and space into some inner box of memory, which may remain locked for years, then suddenly fly open at the breath of lilac or a gust of wind. Association is everything.

Most of Tovey's talk as we walked together on the muddy pavements was beyond me, especially because he so intimidated me, and I was so bent upon looking "interesting", and seeming intelligent, that the effort paralysed my mind. I was still incapable of losing myself even in music; what absorbed me was myself in a musical context. Although what fascinated me about Tovey was his great musicianship, and what I wanted above all was to earn his esteem as a musician, what unwittingly I was striving to do was to capture his affection. At the root of it all was the fear that perhaps I had no musical content worthy of his attention, though the poverty of the material he sometimes had to deal with might give me a relative value; but deeper still, far deeper was the obstinate conviction that something within me was crying out to be born. All this added to my inner confusion. I had succeeded in interesting the great man beyond my wildest expectations – or so it seemed – but just what was that worth since he had never heard me play? I was an acrobat soaring through sidereal space with only the flimsiest net of achievement to succour me in time of need.

As regards my future studies, Tovey gave me sound practical advice, not all of which I was prepared to accept at the time. I wanted to be given the freedom of the world of music, and the assurance that I was fit to settle there. By the magic of his playing he had afforded me an artificial, because unearned, knowledge of that world, such as they say mescaline gives of the world of mystical experience. I was unaware at the time that my initiation was artificial; I believed I had entered that world on legitimate terms. What really he was

now proposing was that I earn the right to live there, by sub-
mitting myself to the hard school of real initiation. He stressed
the importance of a general musical education, not merely
harmony and counterpoint but also fugue, score-reading, history of music, formal analysis, orchestration, composition. He
mentioned them all and my blood ran cold. Would my frail
talent bear so heavy a burden? I had come so late to the real
study of pianoforte technique that it seemed to me I would
barely have time to screw it up to concert standard by giving
my whole time to it. How was I going to master so much else
besides? I had an anguished fear that he doubted my capacity
as a player. I expected every moment to hear from him, too,
the damping suggestion that I take up teaching. But these
were problems which for the moment I could shelve. The
essential point was that I could now tell my father that Tovey
heartily agreed it would be an excellent thing for me to spend
at least a year in Vienna.

In the meantime Letty had gone from school to the
University and I was finding it more and more difficult to take
St. George's seriously. I had long since given up playing all
games except tennis. I was too afraid of breaking my crowned
tooth on a hockey or cricket ball. I still took trouble over my
English essays because I enjoyed writing, but I had trained
myself to sleep during the drowsy afternoon English class, my
forehead resting on my hands above an open book. Of my
waking time, I spent as much as I could reading and dreaming
in the big school library of which I was now librarian, and I
found it more and more difficult to make the effort of getting
to school in time. I had ceased to see my teachers as awful rep-
resentatives of Authority; they had dwindled to mere
vulnerable human beings, and I had with one or two of them
an easy relationship unlike what was then usual between
teacher and pupil. I remember once alighting from the tram-

car in the wake of my English teacher. It was ten minutes past nine, and too late to reach school in time for roll-call. She gave me a friendly smile, and remarked that it was difficult to get to school in time. I agreed, and we walked the rest of the way unhurriedly, talking like friends whom only a difference of age separates. On another occasion my History teacher, the best teacher I ever had, and the first to rouse my interest in History, looked into the classroom where I was sitting putting my books in order at the end of the morning. She said: "I suppose it is no use expecting an essay from you this week?" I answered cheerfully: "Not this week!" Something had come unstuck; and when I look back now, I realize that St. George's was a congenial school in which to develop broadly.

One of the things that did interest me was the German I began to study as soon as it came to seem I would really be going to Vienna. Normally to pass the Higher Leaving Certificate, and be quit of school, required Latin. I was a poor Latin scholar. It had interested me at first so greatly that Margaret and I used to write each other letters in schoolgirl Latin, but after only two years the teacher who had thus galvanised me left. Her place was taken by a Cambridge Double First (so we were told), who had none of her predecessor's dynamism, but was fat, sleepy, and obviously as bored with us as we were with her. It was then I discovered there was a new rule which made it possible to take a second modern language in place of Latin. I appealed to my father, who agreed to my switching over to German; he knew what my Latin was like. Altogether I began to have a fairly easy time. English posed me no problem, French I had learned to speak fluently as a child, and though I was very weak in grammar I had managed to subsist throughout my school years thanks to the capital acquired verbally before the age of ten. My knowledge of Geography was nil, but I was now good at History. As by this

time I had passed my Lower Leaving Certificate, and opted
for a classical or literary formation, I had done with mathe-
matics forever, and that was my real bugbear.

Even so, the prospect of nearly another two years at school
depressed me badly. Work or no work, I had to be present,
and little time was left for practising. Above all, the atmosphere weighed upon me. Now, when I look back on my last
term at school, the magical years that followed shed on those
long lazy summer days a charmed light, and the aching nostalgia I then felt as I gazed from the library windows, or lay
watching the clouds from the grass edge of the playing-fields
where I no longer played, is transmuted by distance into happiness. When we are young we delight in dreaming of the
future, and as we grow older we tend to reverse the same
mechanism and embellish the past; but except in early childhood, or when love heightens and intensifies our perceptive
powers, or during the actual process of creation, the here and
now seldom brings us joy in its own right. In my case, a lack
of inner unity shattered the image of immediate experience. I
had come to believe I hated school, hated Edinburgh, and
almost hated Scotland. I decided that desperate measures were
necessary, and brought all my powers of persuasion to bear on
my father, begging him to convince the school authorities that
I could pass my Higher Leaving Certificate in the Lower,
instead of the Higher, Sixth form. Fortunately for me, he
agreed to do so; even more fortunately, his word had the
weight my achievements might have lacked.

Actually when the time came I succeeded in passing all the
subjects except German. After studying it for only a year my
knowledge was so slight that I remember I translated "umge-
fangen von steilen Klippen" as "fastened together with steel
clips". Again my father found a solution. As the rule then in
vigour did not oblige me to re-sit the examinations I had

passed, he asked the headmistress of another school, a friend of his, to allow me to attend her establishment for German only, which would allow me to sit the examination the following summer. My troubles were over. I would now be able to concentrate solely on music and German, the only subjects which seemed to me to have a bearing on my future.

It was on a wave of unutterable happiness that I made my last appearance within the walls of St. George's School for Girls. The custom of our school was for the top two classes to give a farewell party at the end of the summer term, to which the staff was invited. For those of us who were on the point of leaving, this party took on a special character. Those who had found great happiness at school came to the final scene of their fulfilment in melancholy mood. They were usually the pupils who had shone on the playing-field, and in the gymnasium. Of those who were glad to have done with it all, and who had felt school life as a servitude, I doubt whether any came to that last party in a gladder mood than I. I know I remember that evening as one of the happiest in my life, and I have known many happy evenings. It had been led up to by delightful degrees. There had been the last English class, the last French, the last History, the last everything. The old Bible teacher, Miss Macfarlane, had given us the talk on marriage for which my sisters had prepared me, not without some hilarity. It had taken place exactly as foreseen, beginning with the closing of all windows lest the younger children should hear, and ending in the very words I had been led to expect: "It never came my way girls, but it may come yours. Never marry for money. Never marry for passion. Marry for love!" From first to last not a word had been said that would have been news to the youngest girl in the school. If I had not been warned, I might have found it disappointing.

On the very afternoon of the party I had been to a gathering of Miss Maclachlan's pupils where each had played his or her "piece", and where my performance of Beethoven's C major sonata, opus 2 number 3, had been kept for the end, which made me suddenly realize that she considered me her best pupil. This made me drunk with joy. I had played by heart, and my memory had not failed me as I had feared it would. It was the most I had hoped for. I was modest of my positive attainments, though I was not so modest of what deep in my heart I believed I would one day achieve. I never expected anyone to recognize the latent qualities I imagined I possessed, and I could hardly believe I had come to be anyone's best pupil. So it was that I brought to our farewell party a breast overflowing with gratitude. But I also came to it in a horrid, cocky frame of mind.

Though no young men were to be present at our party – at the time it would have been unthinkable – I had washed my hair and put on my most becoming dress. Round my neck I wore an amber necklace Flora had recently given me, and on my face an expression of studied boredom. I boasted about my playing of the Beethoven sonata, but kept out of reach of the grand pianoforte. I roused envy by telling how in a year I was going to study music in Vienna. I invited the gymnastic teacher to dance with me, as a likely person with whom to show off my dancing. I was odious, but it soon wore off. I was too happy to keep it up.

By the time we had all flocked upstairs to the dining-hall for the feast to which we had each of us brought a contribution, I was a schoolgirl again for the last time, eating like a schoolgirl, chattering like a schoolgirl, giggling like a schoolgirl.

I have often envied Kipling that first return journey to India, or what I imagine it to have been, when he had done with school at last, and was sailing to join his family, not as a child, but as an adult with the prospect of a journalist's job in the country of his birth. What must have been his joy as the ship carried him away from fogs and cruelty, through the rough Bay of Biscay, into the gay Mediterranean, and back at last, through ever hotter days and starrier nights, into his native East. I think I know just what he must have felt. I have only to imagine what I felt myself when I passed the prison walls for the last time, and drove in my taxicab through the pale twilight of our summer night; imagine it expanded and extended to contain his bitterer experiences, and his vaster prospects, his certitude of latent powers, where I had only an obstinate hope, his memories of India, heightened by his dreams, where I had only dreams. He was seventeen; so was I. His was the macrocosm, mine the microcosm. It was as much as I could hold.

CHAPTER SEVENTEEN

Yeats

And so, in September 1922, the last year began which was to lead to the realisation of my childhood's dream of studying music in Vienna. It was a year that brought a good many changes at home. In the course of it, Molly became engaged to be married, Flora graduated from Oxford and went to live and work in London, where she shared a flat with a fellow student from Oxford, Joan Shelmerdine. Alice spent the winter in London, and then went to Holland where an old friend of our father, Ronald Campbell Macfie, poet and medical practitioner, had found her temporary employment in the "Scotch House" on the Island of Veere. The "Scotch House" is an historic house, belonging to Scotland, where exhibitions are – or were – given every summer. Alice's job was to lend a hand to Dr. Macfie's friend, Alma Oakes, then curator, and responsible for the exhibitions. There she made new friends, and we felt that she, too, was slipping away from Scotland. Letty was in her last year at Edinburgh University. She was to go on to Cambridge the following autumn.

Farther afield, Margaret Ludwig – always ahead of me – had passed her final school examinations and gone to Glasgow to study with the best violin teacher there. She and I had hoped to persuade her parents to let her join me in Vienna when the time came, but they were not to be won over. They knew more about the problem than either I or my parents did. No doubt they realized that Margaret, too, lacked the technical grounding which would allow her to make the most of a year abroad. In my own case, in giving the advice he gave, Tovey was viewing the matter from the wider ground of general musical culture. Most of my time was now devoted to practising, and certainly I made some progress; but I was too apt to imagine that the way to acquire what I lacked was by diligent repetition. I believed that by practising four hours a day I was bound to reach my goal, whereas the secret of technical mastery, unless it be a natural gift, is a thing we have to discover for ourselves. A good teacher will set us on the path and guide us at the crossroads, but achievement, when it comes and if it comes, will be in the guise of an intensely personal discovery.

Some progress I did however make, and as I said in the last chapter, Miss Maclachlan believed I had possibilities. She did her best to develop them. When by dint of long practice I brought a piece of music to some degree of finish, she would create opportunities for me to play before a small audience of her pupils. Thanks to her and to Margaret, I even had my share of a modest success. I had introduced Margaret to Miss Maclachlan, who had been as impressed by her gifts as I had hoped and expected, and she had suggested we put our names in for the violin and pianoforte sonata section of the competitive Musical Festival which takes place every year all over Britain. The set piece was Beethoven's A minor sonata, opus 23. I worked hard at my part, and Margaret came over from Glasgow as often as she could to practise our ensemble under Miss Maclachlan's guidance. On the appointed day, sick with the apprehension I never lost when later I did actually come to play in concerts, I followed Margaret onto the platform, and sat down before a hostile-looking instrument. I struck a timid "A", and then, as soon as Margaret had tuned, plunged into the first movement without having given the agreed-on signal.

As in this sonata the two instruments start simultaneously, and in a lively tempo, it might have been fatal. Fortunately Margaret was so quick-witted, and her instrument so well tuned, that she came in only a fraction of a second late. My precipitation did, however, lose us two marks, but we came in first with ninety-eight out of a hundred.

Margaret had all the gifts that go with real musicianship. She had a sense of absolute pitch. She could improvise and play by ear, and she had the inner ear that enables one to read music like a book. I had none of these gifts, though I had a good ear and hands and never lost hope that the rest would develop with time. After all – so I told myself – I had not had the advantage of growing up in a musical family.

Which was all very well, and who knows how I might have developed had I been honest. The truth is that, without going the length of pretending I had the faculties I lacked, I let the thing be supposed, and so wasted both energy and opportunity. Energy, because I was constantly on the alert to avoid the pitfalls that would betray me. Opportunity, because for years I never admitted to Tovey, when later he decided to teach me himself, that I could read in my head only such music as was familiar to me. In other words, that my inner ear depended entirely on my memory. It was then that he explained to me how the inner ear may be developed by building on memory. He advised me to try to read the score of a work immediately after having heard it performed. Here and there the sight of the written music would rouse flashes of memory to the inner ear, and thus, gradually, the link between eye and inner ear would develop to include what one had never heard. But by then it was too late. I had missed my opportunity. There was too much else going on.

On the social side of life our disreputable period had come to an end. When we went to the Palais de Danse it was openly and with "respectable" partners. With Alice away from home there were no parties worth telling of that winter, except for the one our father gave every year for his Honours students, at which we were expected to be present if we happened to be at home. His Honours students were very dear to him, but they interested us not at all. They were inclined to be shy in their professor's presence, which no doubt prevented them from appearing at their best. We had no idea how many interesting personalities there were among them, nor by what a love of poetry they were all possessed.

On the occasion of these parties, my father was at his best and my mother at her sweetest. He joined in all the absurd games that were played in the early stages of the evening to thaw the ice, delighting us all by apostrophising the potatoes in the potato race, as he did all inanimate objects which resisted him; and she, quietly drawing into conversation anyone who seemed left out. She had not an atom of social bluff, but was always her true self with everyone, and she understood shyness because she herself was shy.

We, her children, were thankful to see her so busy, because on the rare occasions when she had made brief appearances at the parties Alice gave, she would sit watching us with on her face an expression of such radiant pride that at last we begged her to keep away, and if possible to keep our father away too. I referred earlier to his habit of selecting the most interesting of the young men down to his study for conversation. He had also a very trying way of taking out his watch to examine it, and then murmuring (audibly): "It waxeth late!" when he grew bored and wanted the guests to leave.

With Alice gone there was, as I said earlier, no more dancing at Twelve Regent Terrace. But her absence had another effect. I was now working hard. The truth is that Alice was something of a disrupting element in my early life. She had a way, around eleven o'clock in the morning, of putting her head round the door of the room where I was busy practising, and saying: "Are you coming down town for coffee and cakes at Crawford's?" Did I ever refuse? I doubt it.

It was not only for her generous nature that I loved her. She was never the bossy elder sister, but always the moving spirit. At the same time, I sensed in her an almost ruthless determination to go her own way, whatever the consequences might involve, and it was this that disturbed and fascinated me. Now that she was gone, my life took a new turn. Instead of going to studio parties I went to as many concerts as possible, those of visiting celebrities, all Tovey's recitals and his concerts with the Reid Orchestra, and I had a season ticket for the Monday Evening Concerts of the Scottish National Orchestra. At the first of these latter concerts I discovered that the seat I had booked was next to that of Dr. Petrie Dunn. I mentioned him earlier, as the man who taught Harmony and Counterpoint at my evening classes. We recognized each other and got into conversation at the first interval. I believe it was on the following Monday that I told him I hoped to take up music seriously and become a pianist. Some instinct prevented me from telling him of my dream of going to Vienna to study. I felt it was all too vague to be exposed to the astute eye of this stout man, well on in his forties, whose florid face would have looked at home in a Bierhalle. And indeed, he had studied in Germany in his youth. His answer was an assenting grunt, but he asked no questions at this stage.

There was another new element in our lives that autumn of 1922. Alice's place had been taken, but only in the spatial sense, for no one could have been more unlike her, by a fellow student of Flora's called Jane. She had come on from Oxford to do research on one Gavin Douglas in the Edinburgh Record Office. To my shame, I do not know to this day who Gavin Douglas was. Somehow Jane never made it clear.

Jane never stopped talking during all the time she was with us, but it was such a gentle flow it was no more disturbing than a summer breeze. Yet I felt that if only I had time to listen I would be carried away on an adventurous journey from tangent to tangent into some strange land (and learn, *en passant*, who Gavin Douglas was). She was at once utterly unselfconscious, and yet delightfully aware of her own absurdity when brought face to face with it. She was a sort of Mélisande, strayed from her native Breton forest to work her magic in the dust of the Edinburgh Record Office. Not that I have any reason to believe there was any dust. All this being so, when Jane returned from a few days' holiday with her family to announce that she was engaged to be married, it came as a shock, a rude awakening from a delectable dream. I remember feeling that to take such a step she must have changed into some more earthly being, and I regretted it. But when I pressed her for more information, and she told me that the condition she had made on agreeing to marry her suitor was that she be given half a crown a week "to squander", I was reassured.

But I have run on ahead of my story.

To return to where I was, the great event of that year was to be the visit of W. B. Yeats. He was to spend several days with us on the occasion of a lecture he was giving, and this time we were to be allowed to meet him, that is to say, Jane, Letty and myself, as being the only ones at home. We already knew a good deal of Yeats' poetry. He was, in fact, the poet whose poetry at that time meant most to me; but it was Jane who fired us to go out, all three, and buy each of us a volume for him to sign. I never at any point could see the value of an author's signature on a book unless the whole thing was a spontaneous gesture; but I was not going to be left out. So out we went, meaning to approach him the next day, when the lecture was over and we met privately.

Actually it was at dinner before the lecture that we first really met him. We were, as usual, tongue-tied, except possibly Jane, but the flow of talk between my father and Yeats took up all the room, and we listened fascinated. We emerged at last from the dining room, all three of us head over heels in love with this beautiful, tall man, with the white forelock in his raven hair and the dreamy forehead and eyes, who believed in fairies as for so long I myself had done, and brought them back to life.

We needed no persuasion to attend his lecture. We had arranged to go with our painter friend, Eric, knowing there would be no room for us in the taxi. We sat as near the platform as we dared, prepared to be enthralled. Unfortunately it was not our father who was to introduce the speaker, but an old friend of his of whom he was fond, because they had been students together, and because they shared the same love of poetry, but whom my sisters and I found extremely irritating. We had heard him introduce speakers on other occasions, and we knew just what to expect. We warned Eric that his opening gambit would be: "When I first met Mr. Yeats face to face", and that he would go on from there to introduce not so much Yeats as himself, enhanced by his links with the great poet. Actually his introductory words were: "When I first met Mr. Yeats in the flesh", and because we were "young and foolish" it was enough, without waiting for what followed, to set us off in an explosion of giggles. Eric sought to silence us, but we only just wiped the tears of laughter from our eyes in time for Yeats himself.

I have forgotten much of what Yeats said, but I do clearly remember his telling us about the messages he gave his subconscious through the agency of certain leaves, which he put under his pillow before going to bed. He was then certain to dream the answer to whatever problem was haunting him. He told us that he once did this when the problem he was up against was "how to win the lady", and how he had made a poem of the dream that came. It was "Cap and Bells", and he read it to us after having given us his explanation of the dream: that women care nothing for a man's soul, or for his heart, but only for his worldly success.

I have forgotten the rest of his lecture, but not one of the poems he read. His reading of poetry was very akin to my father's, with the difference that where the latter had a Scotch accent, Yeats had an Irish lilt. Their voices rang with the same mixture of passion and restraint, both gave to the rhythm its full value – the rhythm, not the beat – but Yeats' reading came nearer to chanting than did my father's. I have still in my ears the long-drawn "Oh-h-h-h" of "Oh, do not pluck at his rein, He is riding to the townland that is the world's bane", which was one of the poems he read. And when at last he read: "Never give all the heart", but left out the last two lines ("He that made this knows all the cost, For he gave all his heart and lost", which I knew by heart), how jealous I was of Maud Gonne!

The next day we were all down in time for breakfast, in a fever of excitement at the prospect of meeting him privately. He came in a little late and we all rose to greet him. It was at this point that, before sitting down, he fixed me with his eye and said: "I was watching you last night, and you looked exactly like Pallas Athene, but you know, you are not her. No young person has wisdom". He went on to say, as he took his place, addressing himself to my parents, that it is a tragic thing when a man reaches the age when he becomes a laughing-stock to the young. It was one of the most miserable moments of my life. No one of us dared to open her lips to tell him the truth, that we had laughed not at him, but at the silliness of the man who had introduced him, and that, far from being a "laughing-stock for the young", he had captured our hearts and minds. We sat with downcast heads and scarlet faces and pretended to eat our breakfast. I did not even hear what answer he was given.

After breakfast he went into the study to work. Neither Letty nor I had the courage to go after him and ask him to sign our books. It was Jane that went. She told him what we wanted, and left the books lying beside him on the desk. We hung hopefully about, and when at last we heard him cross the hall and go out, we rushed down to see what he had written. Letty reached the desk first and chose her book without hesitation. In it Yeats had written: "For wisdom is a butterfly and not a gloomy bird of prey". Jane came next. She chose: "The proud and careless notes live on, But bless our hands that ebb away". What was left for me was: "By the help of an image I call to my own opposite, Summon all that I have handled least, least looked upon". I felt downcast. If I had got the first I could have persuaded myself it had been meant for me, that he had relented. As he knew nothing about me, I could invent for the second quotation no personal intent at all; but other people might, that knew what music meant to me. Poor consolation. As for the third and last quotation, it seemed to me wholly pointless. I had no notion how prophetic it would prove. I was young. I had as yet no experience of Life's implacable sense of humour: "You are quite certain that you will never, whatever the circumstances, do any domestic tasks? Wait and see!"

CHAPTER EIGHTEEN

The Way to Vienna

By this time the musical academic year had come to an end, and Tovey had left Edinburgh for the Spring and Summer. I had really seen very little of him, and on the occasions when he saw me home from the music classrooms I had continued too shy to do more than listen to his flow of talk, not always understanding his sidereal flights. His scope was too vast for me; and anyway, words were not his natural language. More and more the thought that he would surely be disappointed when he heard me play haunted me; I believe now that he had a clearer idea what to expect than I realized, but his vision of what it means to let music into the life of a neophyte with a thirst for it was not bounded by the concert platform. It was a thing always worth doing. However that may have been, I began to be furiously jealous of any and every pianist of my own sex and age who came near him. I remember going to a Reid Concert at which I had been told that an unknown female pianist was going to play. All anyone could tell me was that she was Scotch, and that Tovey had liked her playing and felt she should be given a chance. My place was too far from the platform to allow my short-sighted eyes to discover whether or not my worst fears were justified. In other words, whether she combined what I had with what I lacked. As usual, I was too careful of my appearance to solve the problem by putting on my spectacles. I was so tormented that I even found myself incapable of judging her playing. Anyway, it sufficed to rouse my jealousy that Tovey found her good enough to bring her in front of his public, to play with his orchestra. When the concert was over, as so often before, I invented an excuse to go and see Tovey in the green-room. My sole purpose was to discover whether she was a rival in every sense. What I found was a little elderly lady, or what seemed to me elderly: quiet, modest and unassuming. At the back of my mind a familiar voice murmured: "Not at all handsome. I like her prodigiously". To my relief, Tovey seemed to find it natural that I should have come round after the concert. He even introduced me to the first violin as a future pianist. I went home as radiantly happy as if he had said it "en connaissance de cause". It was presumably the last time I would see Tovey before I left for Vienna and I was glad it had been a happy ending.

And now he was gone. I still saw Dr. Petrie Dunn at the Monday evening concerts, and on the way home from one of them I at last told him I was going to Vienna in the Autumn to study music. I had avoided mentioning it before from an intuition that he would disapprove. I was right. He answered frankly that he thought it a mistake at my present stage. I had admitted to him that I lacked technique and he now said that before going abroad it was essential to have acquired a fair degree of technical mastery, unless one intended to go through the full training of a foreign Conservatoire. If what I intended was to work for a year with some great teachers then I should wait till I was almost at concert level. This shook me badly. I had no idea at all in what conditions I would be studying, nor for how long: whether they would accept me at the Conservatoire or whether I would take private lessons and with whom. No one seemed to know much about who were the best teachers in Vienna at the time. My secret hope was that my parents would finally agree to my staying there for several years, impressed by the progress I expected to make. But now I quailed. Perhaps he was right.

I thought the matter over during the week that followed; but I said nothing to my parents about the new turn events were taking. I was afraid they would immediately decide against Vienna; what Dr. Dunn had said was obviously sensible. Before the next Monday evening I had screwed myself almost to the point of believing I could bear another year in Edinburgh if Dr. Dunn could be persuaded to take me as a pupil. His reputation as a teacher was high. But would he? I was still candid enough to be unaware that a provincial teacher will be glad enough of any intelligent pupil with a real love of music.

And so, on the next occasion of our meeting I told him that if he would take me as a pupil I would postpone going to Vienna. He said he would. The die was cast and I went home feeling very bleak.

I still said nothing to my parents, but the following Sunday I told Miss Maclachlan what I had done. She was furious. She admitted there was some truth in what Dr. Dunn had said, but she too hoped I would be allowed to stay abroad longer than a year. In any case, she felt that Dr. Dunn was an insufficient excuse for leaving her. She did not deny that he was a good teacher "as far as he went", but she said he was not the teacher I needed. I was on the horns of a dilemma. All my longing for Vienna came flooding back and all my desire to be quit of grey Edinburgh. At length Miss Maclachlan suggested I write to Tovey and leave the decision to him, adding that I must be honest about my lack of technique.

On the whole I was glad I was not going to have to face the great man. I knew I would be tongue-tied in his presence but that on paper I would manage better. When, on the following day, I saw Dr. Dunn I told him I had decided I should ask Tovey's advice before making a final decision. After all, it had been his advice I had taken in the first place. He gave an ironical grunt and said I must do as I please, but that Tovey was in Germany and that he never answered letters. This put me on my mettle and when I got home I wrote a letter that began: "Dear Professor Tovey, Dr. Dunn says you never answer letters. Please, please answer this one if only to spite him". The answer came surprisingly promptly and said that though no doubt Dr. Dunn knew more about my situation than he did, he still felt that a year of hearing music in Vienna could only be a good thing, and that he hoped his old friend Dr. Eusebius Mandyczewski would be in some sort the centre of my musical milieu, adding that he was writing to him.

This was beyond anything I had hoped for. I took the letter with me to my next harmony class and showed it to Dr. Dunn. He shrugged his shoulders and said I must do as I please. The way to Vienna was open at last.

I often wonder whether I would have had the courage my parents had when they let me go so far from home alone, so young and in such uncertain conditions. Tovey had given me the name and address of the great musicologist who was then curator of the Musik Verein Museum, but I knew neither where I would live nor with whom I was going to study. So far the only definite arrangement made was that I should join an international summer school which was to take place in Vienna in September, and with whose British members I was to travel from London. The summer school was to last from the ninth of September to the thirtieth. This would give me three weeks during which, with only a schoolgirl's German and a few lines of introduction to an eminent musicologist (which I suspected I would never have the courage to use), I would have to solve my problems for myself.

Now that the decision as regards Vienna was finally made, Miss Maclachlan did her practical best to prepare me to enter, as we supposed, the Vienna Conservatoire. She set me to work at Bach's C minor Prelude and Fugue, Book One, and Schubert's B flat Variations. She made me work hard at my scales and arpeggios, a weak spot. It was only when I reached Vienna that I was to discover the Conservatoire was rivalled by an Akademie. I had to find out which was the better, when the entrance examinations took place and where, and what formalities they would involve. In the meantime, back in Edinburgh, happy in my ignorance, I was undaunted. It was all still a long way off and I was certain that, once safe in the Austrian capital, these problems would solve themselves.

And so the summer term drew to a close. I passed my German examination, the last hurdle between me and my dream.

Early in the summer Molly had come back from visiting Austria with a friend. She had brought with her, I remember, a large variety of building bricks with which I soon discovered I could make better and bigger houses than long ago with the bricks of our childhood. In no time at all the old joy of building gripped me. Flora, too, was back from Oxford. This time she arrived with Puccini's *Madame Butterfly* and set me to sight read the accompaniment to "One fine day". We had an orgy of emotional *laisser-aller*. We were perfectly aware of Puccini's shortcomings, but we enjoyed ourselves immensely, and not only with Puccini but also with such lesser operas as *Cavalleria* and *Pagliacci*.

Unfortunately for me, one sunny afternoon when I had just built a magnificent house on the grand pianoforte in our drawing-room overlooking Holyrood Palace, and in my joyful satisfaction was serenading it with Madame Butterfly's Love Duet, my foot firmly resting on the pedal, the door opened and the maid announced: "Professor Tovey". I remember that I gasped: "My God, how awful!" and buried my face in my hands till his entering the room forced me to pull myself together. That he should hear me thus for the first time! He made no remark on what I had been doing, but there was a gleam of laughter in his eyes that was not reassuring. He came, however, straight to the point, telling me he had me on his conscience and, happening to be in Edinburgh, had come to see how things were shaping as regards Vienna. I remember nothing more, except that he admired the house I had built. My mind was in too great a turmoil. I think my parents came home and took him off my hands. I did not see him again till he suddenly turned up in Vienna the following October and took me himself to call on Dr. Mandyczewski, where I had not yet dared to go; and also to the rehearsal of a concert Fritz Busch was conducting with the Vienna Philharmonic. Better than all, he took me to call on old Clara Wittgenstein, the philosopher's favourite aunt, as I said earlier, who had been one of the chief centres of music before the First World War. It was she especially who became the axis round which my musical world revolved, an advantage for which I have never ceased to be grateful.

Soon after Tovey's visit we left for Dinnet. I have only the vaguest recollections of that summer. I remember that the Ludwigs were there, in the rooms they had rented in the village of Ordie, and that Violet had much to tell us about the London School of Music where she was now studying, and Margaret about her musical life in Glasgow. Grandpapa and Aunt Flora must certainly have been at Glendavan. I forget what other people were there and which of my sisters. Only one thing stands out clearly in my memory, the visit that Lord and Lady Aberdeen paid my parents one afternoon. No doubt they had been calling on my grandfather and looked in at our cottage on their way back. They were both interested in my father.

Lady Aberdeen was a tremendous old lady and a great supporter of Women's Rights. Their visit was important enough to stay in my memory if only because when Lady Aberdeen learned that I was going to Vienna she offered to send me introductions to some of her Viennese friends. She was as good as her word. Before I left I received three letters: one for the wife of the Austrian Minister of Finance, one to a delightful lady called Frau Mully-Markl, who proved very helpful, and one to the mother of Herr Hainisch, the then President of Austria.

I did not, when the time came, benefit by these letters as much as I might have done. It was not till some months had passed, under pressure from Alice, who had joined me and was studying applied art, that I nerved myself to disturb such important people, by which time the thick envelopes with their coronets had suffered a little from their long sojourn in a drawer. I remember all the same having tea in Madame Hainisch's drawing-room with a large gathering and being especially interested to meet the sister of Fritz Kreisler, the great violinist of the time. But though I made little use of the letters, they served their purpose by giving my parents the feeling that I was confronting Vienna under excellent auspices.

At the end of August we returned to Edinburgh and I began my farewell visits. One was to Raffalovich. When we said our final "good-bye" he spoke the words he was to speak every time I came to pay a farewell visit before each of my successive departures for Vienna. With his strong Russian accent he would beg me: "And dear child, don't marry some horrrible forrreigner!" I did worse by his standards. I married a Huguenot.

I paid a last visit too to Eric and Cecile. There were few people present that evening. One of them was a beautiful sophisticated American woman, probably twice my age,

whom Eric was painting. When she saw my radiant face and
learned its cause she said: "How lucky you are to be so happy
simply because you are going somewhere!" I never forgot it.
Somewhere it struck a chill; but the memory of her words,
and especially the tone of her voice helped to keep alive in me
right up till now the faculty of being happy "simply because I
was going somewhere". I have a last curious recollection, one
I can fit into no context but which remains as clear as clear in
my memory: that shortly before I left, Yeats called on us; but
how could that be? Certainly he was not staying in the house,
but I remember my mother bringing him upstairs to the
drawing-room where I chanced to be, and telling him that I
was leaving in a few days to study music in Vienna. I know,
because I remember it as a sort of liberation; I was so possessed
by the joy of what was before me that quite suddenly I ceased
to be shy of him. I remember nothing more.

I was to spend a few days with Flora and Joan in London
before starting on the long train journey through Paris to
Vienna. For some post-war reason which was never clear to
me the route through Germany was banned in 1923; and so I,
who had never left Scotland, was to get my first sight of the
three great capitals of Europe in the course of a few days.
Though of Paris I saw only a few streets as we drove from one
station to the other, Flora showed me as much of London as
she could in the short time we were together. We visited
Lincoln's Inn and we lunched at the Cheshire Cheese. We
dined in a Chinese restaurant and we went to the theatre to
see the *Beggars' Opera*, then the rage in Britain. Finally both
Flora and Joan took me to the station, but we missed by five
minutes the train that contained what were to have been my
fellow travellers. It was a bad moment, but they arranged for
some official to telephone ahead that I would join the convoy
at Boulogne. And so I was rushed to another train on the

point of starting, and left alone to face my first feeling of disquiet about the whole undertaking.

The rest?

The rest, except for experience of living under enemy occupation during the last war, the rest is Private Life.

Index

Index

Index